FIBERARTS DESIGN BOOK THREE

Cover: Detail of FLIGHT *by Yael Bentovim. Airbrushed handmade paper; cotton linter, shredded sisal: 55 by 50 inches.*

Copyright © 1987, 1991 by Lark Books

Fiberarts Design Book Three
I. Textile crafts. 2. Fiberwork. I. Mathews, Kate.
II. Title: Fiberarts Design Book Three

Published in 1987 by:
 Lark Books
 50 College St.
 Asheville, North Carolina 28801, U.S.A.

Printed in Hong Kong

ISBN 0-937274-61-5

FIBERARTS DESIGN BOOK THREE

EDITED BY KATE MATHEWS

Lark Books
Asheville, North Carolina

FIBERARTS DESIGN BOOK THREE

EDITOR:
Kate Mathews

ART DIRECTOR:
Rob Pulleyn

TYPESETTER:
Eric Woro
Sandra Soto

PRODUCTION:
Tracy D. Hyorth
Thom Boswell

VALUABLE ASSISTANCE:
Mary Marvel
Pat Wald
Darren Craine
Poche Carter

PUBLISHER:
Rob Pulleyn

CONTENTS

INTRODUCTION 6

TAPESTRY 9

TWO DIMENSIONS 41

THREE DIMENSIONS 69

PAPER AND FELT 81

BASKETRY 97

QUILTING 111

SURFACE DESIGN 141

NEEDLEWORK 155

DIVERSIONS 171

WEARABLES 179

INDEX 203

INTRODUCTION

The introductions to the first two Fiberarts Design Books reported primarily on the sheer magnitude of such an undertaking: the thousands of slides and photos, the long hours spent viewing submitted works, reviewing, contemplating, debating, compromising, organizing, and reorganizing. While the same process took place for this book, we were prepared for it. We were accustomed to mail sacks full of entries arriving each day and the clerical nightmare of processing every submission. We knew we would be fearful of giving an incorrect photo credit or, horror of horrors, showing a piece upside down. We expected to be gloriously surprised by seeing quality work we hadn't seen before, and we were. As with the two previous books, we smiled with a deep sense of satisfaction when we finished.

It has been seven years since the publication of the first Fiberarts Design Book, thirteen years since the first issue of *Fibercraft News*, later to be named *Fiberarts*, and twenty years since we first became involved in fiber ourselves, as craftsmen and enthusiasts. Only now do we feel prepared to make some observations about the development of the fiber arts from their early days during the late 1960s "crafts boom" to the book you're holding in your hands.

Innovative experimentation with textile techniques had been explored since the 1950s by a handful of artists in Europe and the United State and their works set exciting precedents for contemporary textile trends. But during the late 1960s a convergence of sociological changes created a broader-based interest in weaving, dyeing, quilting, needlework, and other crafts.

Many people see the genesis of today's fiber scene in the counterculture movement of the 1960s. They remember tribes of young people living communally, tie-dyeing and weaving fabric, embroidering blue jeans, and spinning yarn from their own sheep, goats, rabbits, or dogs. The era became known for creative street fashion and unconventional use of traditional materials. This may have spurred some interest, but a more important cultural development was the liberation of women from the role of homemaker. With more leisure time, disposable income, education, and exposure to other contemporary art forms, women felt a growing need to express themselves creatively. Because of familiarity with fabrics and yarns in their domestic roles, many women turned to fibers as a natural choice of media.

All of a sudden, local community colleges and large universities alike began offering textile craft courses, fiber supply shops and galleries opened up in the smallest of towns, craft fairs were born, and local museums started exhibiting crafts of all media. This popular movement also spawned new craft supliers, publishers, and guilds. Crafts seemed to be everywhere—in magazine advertising, church bazaars, interior decorating, and even on television.

In the late 1970s, a short ten years later, the "boom" was over, but interest and commitment remained on a smaller scale. While schools began restricting or eliminating textile curricula, mainstream publishers moved on to other fads, and some fiber supply shops closed down, committed fiber artists were quietly cultivating and pruning their work. The dabblers dropped out, leaving a dedicated crowd of textile aficionados who proudly realized they had a decade of experience behind them.

The first Fiberarts Design Book, published in 1980, reflected this dedication to fibers as expressive media and documented the exciting cross-pollination of techniques. The tapestry maker also wove baskets, the surface designer went 3-D into sculptured fabric, and the papermaker embellished with needlework. Artists forged ahead in many new directions, seeking fresh combinations of technique; they were not intimidated by the untraditional, unusual, or unacceptable. During these experimental times results were sometimes awkward and uncontrolled, but the struggle to harmonize technique, medium, and artistic message was all-important.

When the second Fiberarts Design Book was published in 1983, it appeared that a kind of retrospection had set in. Artists pulled back from the exhilarating multimedia frontier and painstakingly contemplated traditional styles and methods. Mastery of the fiber "palette" was sought, so the creative product could be purposefully orchestrated rather than left to chance. Artists gained skillful control over the tools of their trades *and* their aesthetic visions.

This third edition presents the fruits of innovation bred with concentrated technical study. The works in this book, all created in the last four years, exhibit considerable sophistication and maturity; each one, in its own way, pays distinct tribute to the pioneers of the 1950s and the succeeding years of evolution. Each is also just one small step in its maker's growth, a harbinger of visions yet to be captured and expressed.

The first Fiberarts Design Book was dedicated to all those who submitted work, whether accepted or not. The second was dedicated to all those who enjoy textiles, artists or not. This *Fiberarts Design Book Three* is dedicated to all those who have contributed to the cause—the teachers, shop owners, publishers, and gallery owners who believed; the spouses, children, and lovers who went without dinner and still gave moral support; and the friends who didn't understand but still encouraged. You can all take a look at today's fiber art and smile with a sense of participation and accomplishment. Thanks.

The Fiberarts Staff
September, 1987

TAPESTRY

Christine Benson
Dancer
Woven tapestry; wool, rayon; 50
by 72 inches.

A

A

Marcel Marois
Les Angles d'un Site
High warp woven tapestry; natural wool; 126 by 170 inches. Photo: Jean-Rene Archambault.

B

Tricia Goldberg
Burano
Woven tapestry; wool, cotton; 96 by 29 inches. Photo: Dan Dosick.

C

Liv Pedersen
Stampede
Woven tapestry on Dutch plank loom; 56 by 36 cm., each panel.

Deann Joy Rubin
Boccie Ball
Woven tapestry; cotton, wool, cowhair; 35 by 40 inches. Photo: Michael H. Rubin.
This piece deals with the creation of space and the abstraction of the figure. It uses the same two figures defined only by light and shadow with color.

E

Christine T. Laffer
Pacific Stock Exchange
Woven tapestry; wool, cotton; 115 by 62 inches. Photo: Jacques Cressaty.

B

C

D

E

A
Christine T. Laffer
Earl's Court, 5 pm
Woven tapestry; wool, cotton; 30 by 63 inches. Photo: Victor Budnik.

This piece is about many things, yet the strongest thing I wanted to convey was stopping a moment in time, where a viewer is caught between wanting to stop to contemplate and wanting to hurry by.

B
Barbara Heller
Through the Archway
Woven tapestry; linen, wool, cotton, rayon; 46 by 59 inches.
One of a series revealing the spirits in the stones.

C
Stephen Thurston
Entrada
Woven tapestry, wrapping, hand tufting; wool, silk, mohair, cotton, linen, rayon, metallic; 6 by 9 feet. Photo: Steincamp / Ballogg.
This tapestry was inspired by the doorways in Venice, Italy.

D
Rita Romanova Gekht
Somewhere in the Past
Woven tapestry; wool; 48 by 30 inches.
Abstracted perspective and shading of colors create an illusion of space.

E
Alison Keenan
The Open Gate
Gobelins tapestry; wool, cotton; 66 by 47 inches. Photo: Barbara Cohen.

A

B

A
Sandra Kay Johnson
Tales of the Arabian Nights
Woven tapestry; wool, silk, linen; 103 by 86 inches.

B
Care Standley
Stripes
Woven tapestry; wool, silk, cotton; 41 by 21 inches.

C
Constance Hunt
Sisters-A Family Portrait
Woven tapestry; wool, cotton; 64 by 48 inches. Photo: Gary Hunt.

When the cartoon for this tapestry was finished, it was pointed out to me that a number of my family's intimate details had worked their way into the design: the three queens equal the three daughters, the five of hearts my mother, the face down card my dead father.

D
Susan L. Hoover
Aulikki
Swedish knot tapestry; cotton metallic threads; 7 by 3¼ inches.

C

D

A

Deborah Hildreth

Sagg Store

Gobelins tapestry; wool, cotton, silk; 46 by 29 inches. Photo: Sarah Wells.

B

Cindy Lowther

Courthouse

Woven tapestry; wool, cotton; 5 by 4½ feet. Photo: Richard Rodriguez.

C

Ruth C. Manning

Thursday—Garbage Day in the Wedge

Woven tapestry, embroidery; wool, cotton; 44 by 23 inches. Photo: Steven Roussel.

I have always loved working with buildings. When the morning announcer for our public radio station began starting his Thursday show with the words, "Today is Thursday, garbage day in the Wedge," I knew I had a tapestry to make.

D

Tina Sutton

Paradise Lost

Weft-face weaving, discontinuous weft, dyeing; silk, boucle wool; 104 by 184 cm.

E

Gugger Petter

Stairs

Natural wools; 43 by 79 inches. Photo: Claude Hannaert.

I am inspired by details of daily life, light, shadow, and perspective.

A

B

16

C

D

E

A

Victor Jacoby
Calendula
Woven tapestry; cotton, wool;
41 by 41 inches. Photo: James
Toms.

B

Gabrielle Sutt
Trilliums
Gobelins tapestry; cotton, wool;
72 by 48 inches. Photo: M. Sutt.

C

Karen Leitch
The Gardener's Cats
Gobelins tapestry; wool, silk,
cotton, linen; 33 by 48 inches.

D

Sara Hotchkiss
Madd Apple Mandela
Woven tapestry; cotton fabric,
cotton; 36 by 38 inches. Photo:
Stretch Teummler.

*This piece was commissioned
and woven for a friend who
owned the Madd Apple Cafe. In
designing the piece, I was
inspired by her personality, her
attitude toward cooking, and
the interior space it was to
hang in.*

E

C. Elizabeth Smathers
Snowstorm Crocus
Woven tapestry; handspun,
vegetable dyed wools, linen;
56½ by 50 inches. Photo:
Richard Smathers.

*This tapestry was inspired by
the stamen of a Snowstorm
crocus magnified to the point of
non-recognition.*

F

Myra Reichel
Miroian Dream
Inlaid tapestry; wool, silk,
cotton, synthetics, metallics; 78
by 33 inches. Photo: Rick
Echelmeyer.

A

B

C

D

E

F

A

Anthea Mallinson
West Coast Sun God
High warp Gobelins tapestry; wool, cotton, lurex; 104 by 91 cm.

B

Norma Szumski
River Force
Gobelins tapestry; wool, cotton; 46 by 31 inches. Photo: A. J. Szumski.

C

Deborah Hickman
Pangnirtung Pass, View III
Woven tapestry, cotton, wool; 45 by 17 inches.

This tapestry was inspired by the scenery at Pangnirtung, Baffin in Canada's north, where I spent three years as the manager of a weaving center for Inuit tapestry weavers.

D

Louise Weaver Greene
Cathedral
Woven tapestry; wool, linen; 81 by 60 inches.

The silent timelessness of trees in the woods reminds me, in their soaring verticals and steep diagonals, of the lines of Gothic architecture, and the play of light and shadow among the trunks and foliage of the sun on stained glass.

A

B

C

D

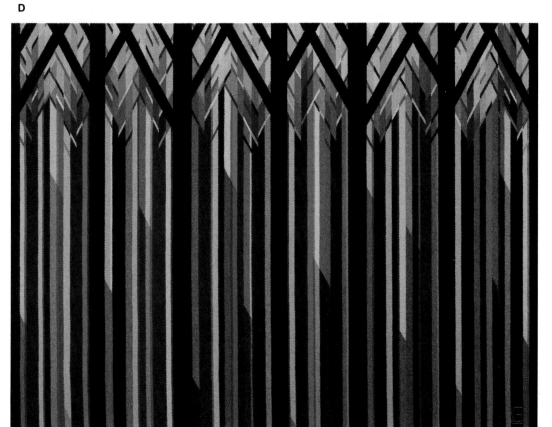

E

Janet Crafer

Lily Pond

Gobelins tapestry; wool, cotton; 80 by 80 cm.

The point of departure for my designs is often landscape and the influence of the weather on the scene. My imagination is often fired by what cannot always be seen: forces of the elements like pressure domes, fronts, and anti-cyclones. Water, as an element, is prominent in much of my work, appearing as waves on the sea, ripples in a pond, or rain falling gently through clouds.

F

Janet Crafer

Gate

Gobelins tapestry; wool, cotton; 100 by 80 cm.

More recently, I have been looking closer at my surroundings. The garden, itself my own creation, provides an endless source of material. A tapestry design is sometimes a development of a new garden feature, or a young plant growing and filling a space.

E

F

A

B

C

D

F

A
Christine Benson
Lawnchair Women
Woven tapestry; wool, cotton, rayon; 72 by 96 inches.

B
Elene Gamache
L'Autre Moi
High warp tapestry; wool, rayon, cotton, metallized acrylic; 39 by 51 inches. Photo: Claire Morel.

C
Dean Johns
Nick and Tig at Tybee
Slit tapestry; wool blends; 28½ by 41 inches.

D
Barbara Heller
Hella Ophelia
Woven tapestry; linen, wool, silk, cotton, rayon; 44½ by 62 inches.
One of a series revealing the spirits in the stones.

E
Jenny Kathleen Cook
The Conversation
Gobelins tapestry; wool, cotton; 137 by 122 cm.
The human figure is the departure point for ideas. The work is concerned with the forces of life: tension, weight, rhythm, and movement.

F
Elene Gamache
Le Chat Marcel
High warp tapestry; wool, rayon, cotton, metallized acrylic; 133 by 97 inches. Photo: Claire Morel.

A

A
Susan Kelly
Red Boots
Woven tapestry; cotton, wool;
49 by 26 inches.

B
Susan Kelly
A Fish Out of Water
Woven tapestry; cotton, wool; 7
by 7 feet.

*Whimsy and humour, some-
times with a sense of mystery,
are the elements with which I
like to work in a somewhat
graphic style.*

B

C

C
Ilona Mack
Wedding
Gobelins tapestry; cotton, wool; 3 by 8 feet. Photo: Tom Flynn.

D
Sharon Marcus
Lex
Gobelins tapestry; wool, cotton, gold, metallic; 34 by 25½ inches. Photo: Bill Bachhuber.
I am increasingly fascinated with the narrative potential of tapestry and because of this seek to produce tapestries with the types of images which invoke a sense of wanting to "know the story behind the work."

E
Claudia Mederer
Tree 1
Gobelins tapestry; silk, linen; 55 by 55 cm.
I try to show processes and structures in nature in a fantastic and colorful way.

F
Barbara Heller
Fold Along the Dotted Line Series: Vancouver Takeout
Woven tapestry; linen, wool; 18 by 15 inches.
This is from a series of seven pieces that begins with a landscape, then a map of the greater Vancouver area, and then focuses down to the last one, which is the floor plan of my studio.

D

E

F

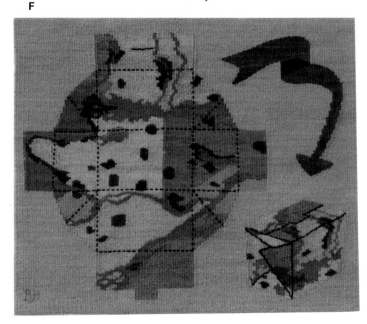

A

Julie McCracken

Pas-de-deux

Woven tapestry; wool, silk; 3 by 2 feet. Photo: Custom Graphics.

I enjoy designing repeating patterns, using a variety of colors and textures.

B

Scott Hendricksen

Untitled

Interlock tapestry; wool, linen; 64 by 40 inches.

C

Kathleen L. Kent

Software

Woven tapestry; wool, mohair, cotton; 55 by 40 inches. Photo: Craig Overbeck.

This design was inspired by a photograph of a computer chip.

D

Deane M. Wernet

Border II

Interlock tapestry; wool, linen; 44 by 65½ inches. Photo: J. Benedetto.

In a series of woven rugs, I am attempting to rethink and expand on the traditional methods of integrating the outer edge with the inner space of the work.

E

Ellen Athens

Wedge Weave Sunset

Tapestry, wedge weave, twill; cotton, wool, rayon; 24½ by 18 inches.

A

B

C

D

E

A

B

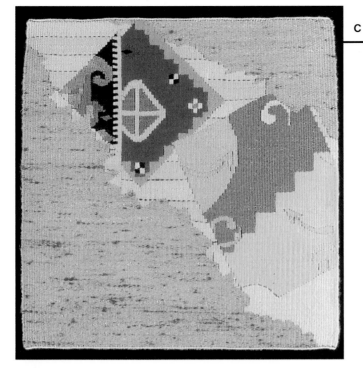

C

A

Kristin Carlsen Rowley
J. At Artpark
Woven tapestry; wool, linen; 14 by 50 inches.

B

Dilys Stinson
Caribbean Squares
Gobelins tapestry; wool, cotton, silk, linen; 61 by 89 inches.
I am concerned with the particular qualities of the tapestry itself: intensity of color, textural qualities, surface rather than line. The inspiration comes from many sources, but often the origin is a passing comment in conversation with a friend or colleague.

C

Lynn Basa
World View
Gobelins tapestry, slit warp variation; silk, cotton, wool, linen, metallic thread; 8 by 8 inches. Photo: IMS-UW.

D

Donna Martin
Last Night's Dream
Woven tapestry; vegetable dyed wool, mohair; 37½ by 55 inches. Photo: Steve Piersol.

E

Ilze Aviks
Fairy Tale
Interlock and dovetail tapestry; wool, linen; 4 by 7 feet. Photo: John Mahoney.

D

E

A

Odette Brabec
After the Storm
Slit tapestry; wool, metallics, rayon, silk, cotton; 72 by 54 inches.

B

Ulrika Leander
Flowing to the Sea
Woven tapestry, soumak; wool, cotton, metallic; 450 by 150 cm. Photo: J.R. Rodgers, Oliver Springs.
This piece shows the serene continuity of changes in nature.

C

Dana Loud
Lady Liberty
Woven tapestry; wool, seine cotton; 17¼ by 19½ inches. Photo: Dan Lawless.
. . . to create the richness of volume and depth through the illusion of flowing curves in a system bound by verticals and horizontals . . .

D

Boyana H. Leznicki
Aquarium
Woven tapestry; wool; 135 by 160 cm.

E

David L. Johnson
Portrait of the Wiggly Man
Woven tapestry; cotton, wool; 30 by 47 inches.
I came to tapestry weaving after being a musician for many years. Both the process and product of my work are analogous to music in my thinking.

F

Judi Maureen White
Spirit Pathways Series #4: Soaring
Two- and three-dimensional tapestry, brocade; wool, linen, silk, metallic, rayon; 46 by 66 by 3 inches. Photo: Bill Lorenz.
The three-dimensional elements represent manmade creations casting shadows and even penetrating (or leaving vacant openings) the two-dimensional tapestry forms that represent land. This expresses, in a direct way, my view of the conflicts that often occur as a result of man's use of the land.

A

B

C

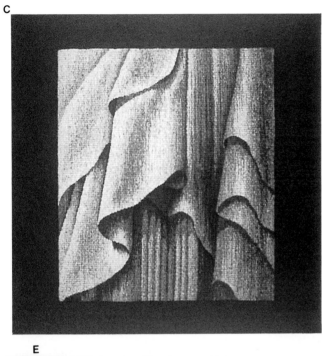

D

E

F

A

Murray Gibson

Oasis

Slit tapestry; wool, silk, rayon, cotton seine twine; 58 by 58 inches.

B

Ann Newdigate Mills

Those Who Stayed

Gobelins tapestry; natural and synthetic fibers; 7 by 1 feet. Photo: Grant Kernan.

By choosing to work in Gobelins tapestry to depict the female body, I hope that I might be able to challenge some stereotypes concerning art, virtue, and other concerns relating to the human condition.

C

Sue Lawty

Haworth Moor

Woven tapestry; wool, linen, cotton; 3 by 2 meters. Photo: Charlie Meecham.

Haworth Moor is Bronte country—rough stone walls and open moorland, the sort of landscape which inspires me. This piece was commissioned for the new British High Commission building in Accra, Ghana—a little piece of England in West Africa.

D

Nancy Belfer

Nazca Journey

Woven, painted, stitched; 71 by 31 inches. Photo: Philip Gerace.

A

B

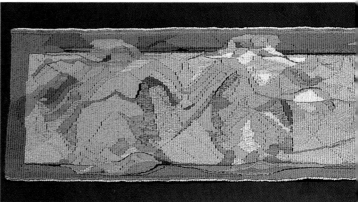

C

D

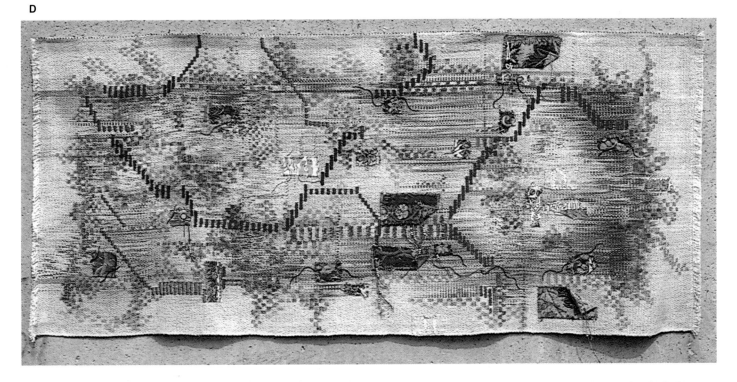

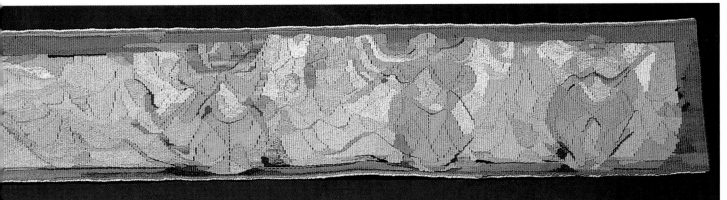

A

B

Oh, had I a Golden Thread and a Needle so fine
I would weave a Magic Strand of Rainbow Design...

In it I would weave the Bravery of Women giving Birth...

And in it I would weave the Innocence of Children of all the Earth...

Show my Brothers and Sisters my Rainbow Design
I would bind up this sorry world with Hand and Heart and Mind...

C

34

D

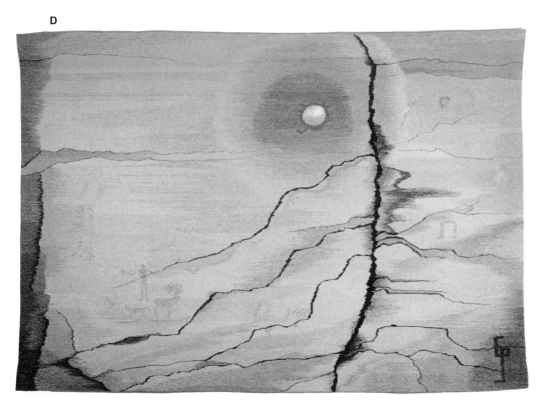

E

A

Michele R. Hamrick

Hot Summer Night/Red Light

Woven tapestry; wool, mohair, linen; 65 by 81 inches.

B

Kathy Spoering

Oh, Had I a Golden Thread . . .

Woven tapestry, embroidery, quilting; wool, cotton, metallics; 28 by 28 by 1 inches. Photo: Karen Kunzelman.

Inspired by Pete Seeger's song of the same title, this piece is a personal reminder of the Ribbon project.

C

Ulrika Leander

Gennesaret

Woven tapestry, soumak; wool, cotton; 53 by 106 inches. Photo: Paul Hester.

This piece, with 12 boat-shaped arches, was commissioned for the Norwegian Seamen's Church in Houston, Texas.

D

Gabrielle Sutt

Indian Rockpainting

Gobelins tapestry; wool, cotton; 72 by 48 inches.

E

Midori Nagai

Apartment

Woven tapestry; wool, cotton, linen; 56 by 38 inches. Photo: David Saltmarche.

A

Theodora Elston
In and Out

Woven tapestry; wool, silk, linen; 70 by 59 inches.

I was thinking about color migration and changing moods as I wove this piece.

B

Ruth Bilowus Butler
An Aztec Two-Step Kind of Night

Woven tapestry; perle cotton, silk; 5 by 6 inches.

C

Midori Nagai
Windowscape

Woven tapestry; wool, cotton, linen; 42 by 57 inches. Photo: David Saltmarche.

A

C

B

D

D

Joanne Soroka
Fifth Business

Woven tapestry; wool, linen, cotton; 78 by 70 inches. Photo: Ian Southern.

This piece was inspired by a performance of Henry V and by the theatrical use of streaming banners and dry ice clouds.

E

Sherry Owens
Surface Break

Slit tapestry; wool, silk, linen, lurex; 72 by 48 inches.

E

A

Denise Marie Kraft

Intersecting Parallel Dimensions

Three-shaft tapestry; wool, cotton; 38 by 48 inches. Photo: Red Carson.

B

Barbara Schulman

Palindromes

Woven tapestry; linen; 95½ by 15 inches. Photo: Doug Van de Zande.

C

Margarete Pfaff

Hoffnung

Kelim tapestry; wool; 96 by 120 cm.

I want to express that, even in dark moments, hope and light exist.

D   p.38-39/026-C

Vera K. Worling

Paths Not Taken

Gobelins tapestry; wool, linen; 47 by 36½ inches.

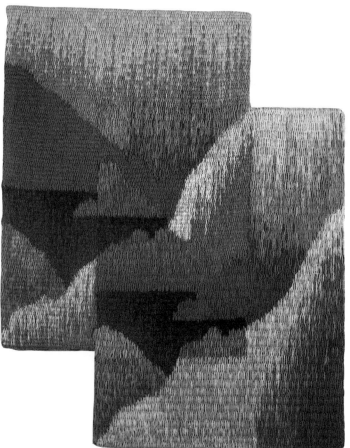

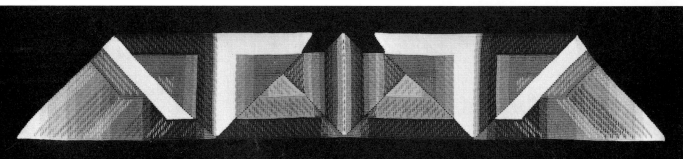

C

D

A

Tricia Goldberg and Bonni Boren
Untitled Abstract
Woven tapestry; wool, cotton; 44 by 57 inches. Photo: Al Marshall.

B

Henry Easterwood
Red Garden XVII
Woven tapestry; wool, linen; 7 by 5 feet.

A

B

TWO DIMENSIONS

Barbara Walker
Untitled
Twill, brocade, inlay, own technique; linen, cotton; 32 by 48 inches. Photo: Jack Ramsdale.

A

Sine McCann
Dark Side of the Mesh
Wire wrapped with cotton threads; 29 by 35 cm.

B

Karen Chapnick
Unfamiliar Landmarks
Interlocking braiding; fabric, textile paints; 60 by 46 inches. Photo: Henri Robideau.

C

Molly Hart
Rain Forest
Strips of copper foil handwoven horizontally, stainless steel and mylar woven vertically, with hand-tied wire; 36 by 47 by 2½ inches.

D

Hyun Mi Jang
Turning Point
Woven and plaited strips of linen and mixed fabrics; 26 by 29 inches.

E

Jennifer Moore
Prism Break
Doubleweave pick-up; cotton; 12 by 13 inches. Photo: William Dewey.

A

B

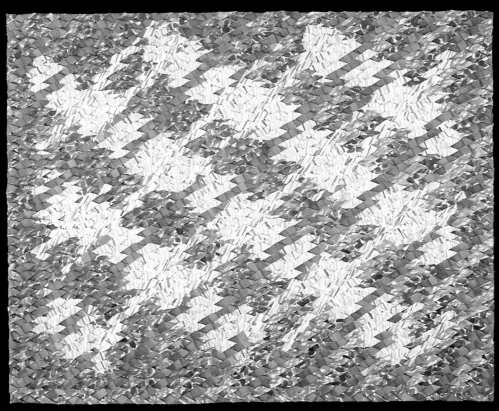

C

E

F
Dona Rozanski
Square Dancing
Inlay; cotton sewing and crochet threads; 12 by 12 by ½ inches.

D

F

43

A

B

C

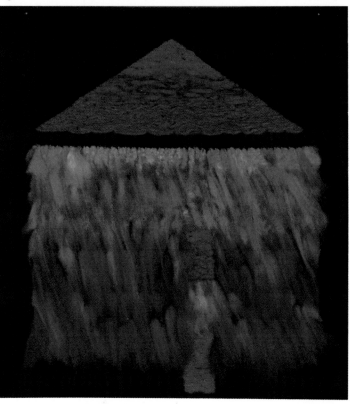

A
Susan D. Wilchins
Beneath the Feet of Dancing Flowers
Dyed, pieced, appliqued, and stitched cotton fabrics; 32½ by 30½ by 1 inches. Photo: Marc Wilchins.

B
Hyun Mi Jang
Spring Fever
Machine-stitched, plaited strips of silk and mixed fabrics; 33 by 33 inches.

C
Leena O'Connor
Road to the Baca
Twisted poppana, brushed wool, cotton; 36 by 38 inches. Photo: Harold O'Connor.
This piece is inspired by the intense sunsets of the San Luis Valley of southern Colorado.

D
Aafke Stavenga
Grass III
Starched and painted cotton and silk; 22 by 22 by 12 cm, each.

E
Kay Campbell
Caravelas Bay
Stitched, gathered, manipulated assemblage; silk fabric, rayon and metallic fibers, wood, acrylic; 36 by 48 by 1 inches, each. Photo: Frank Foster.
My interest focuses on transmitting images such as rippling fields or the crests of waves on water surfaces. I have recently been incorporating the use of abstracted map imagery.

A

B

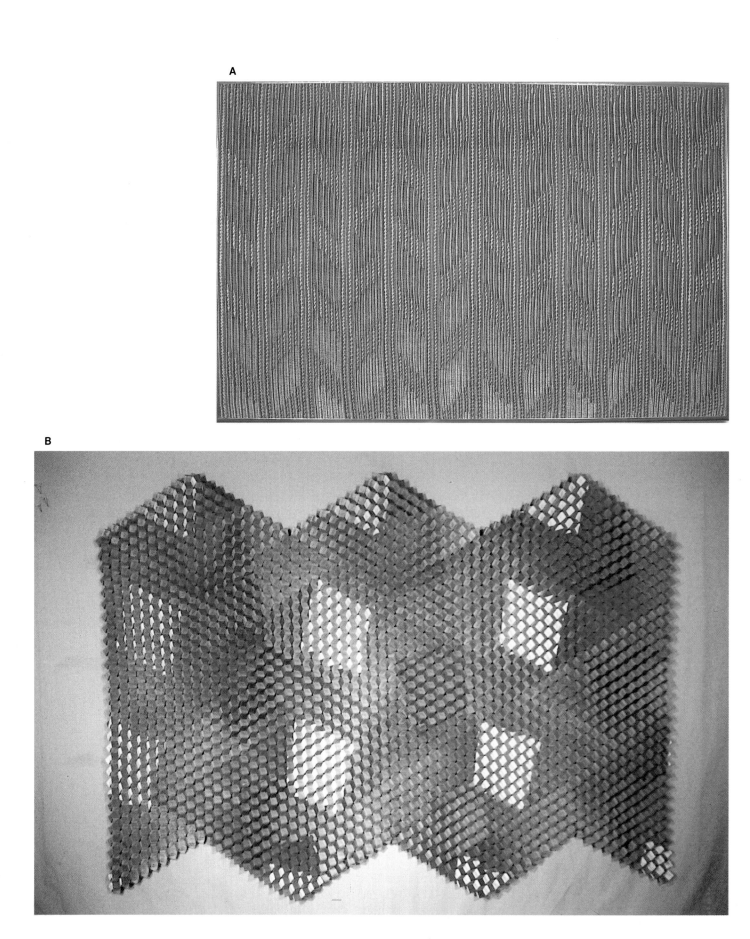

A
Ruth Gowell
Untitled
Warp face weave; hand-dyed rayon, nylon monofilament, electrical cord; 32 by 21 by 1 inches.
There are three layers of rayon in this piece and I was interested in the color interactions which take place.

B
Sherri Smith
Ghost Squares
Plaiting; cotton webbing; 7 by 4½ feet.

C
Patti Mitchem
Frolic
Warp rep weave; cotton; 48 by 54 inches.

D
Cynthia Neely
Aerial Boundaries
Three-color block weave with shaft-switching; wool, silk, rayon, linen; 5 by 4 feet. Photo: John Pelverts.
Diagonals and color shading evoke a sense of movement, space, and dimension.

D

A

B

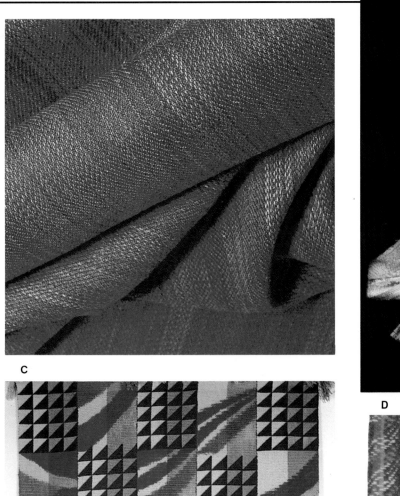

C

D

A
Fran Mather
Silken Twill
Hand-dyed twill fabric; silk, cotton; 45 inches wide. Photo: Barrett Rudich.

B
E. Del Zoppo
Spring Pink Scarf
Damask weave; douppioni silk; 77 by 77 cm.

C
Isis Ray
African Famine
Painted warp, silk screen, weaving; linen, cotton, fiber reactive dyes; 38 by 71 inches.

D
Wanda Clayton James
Deco Progression
Computer-designed weave; wool, metallic thread; 30 by 65 inches.

E
Terri Hall
Tikal
Supplementary warp weave; hand-dyed silk, polyester, nylon, metallic yarn, ribbon; 35 by 85 cm. Photo: Brett Martin.

F
Kaija Sanelma Harris
Mirage Three
Four-harness doubleweave; cotton, wool; 49 by 79 by 1 inches. Photo: Grant Kernan, A.K. Photos.

E

F

A

B

C

D

E

A

Karen R. Gutowski

Northern Lights

Weft face weave, shaft-switching; wool, linen; 24 by 40 inches. Photo: Mats Nordstrom.

I enjoy playing with the patterns and colors to create a movement and spatial quality within the flat woven surface.

B

Connie Kindahl

East Mountain #2

Boundweave on overshot threading; wool, linen; 3 by 5 feet.

C

Doris Louie

Rug

Woven tapestry; wool, linen; 36 by 66½ inches. Photo: Untitled Fine Arts.

D

Barbara Walker

Carnival

Twill, brocade, inlay, and own techniques; linen, cotton; 60 by 33 inches. Photo: Peter Hogan.

My work is concerned with the layering of marks and rays of color on different planes; of transposing one field on top of another, and the interaction each individual plane has with one another.

E

Cynthia Neely

Passage

Three-color block weave with shaft-switching; wool, linen; 6 by 4 feet. Photo: John Pelverts.

A

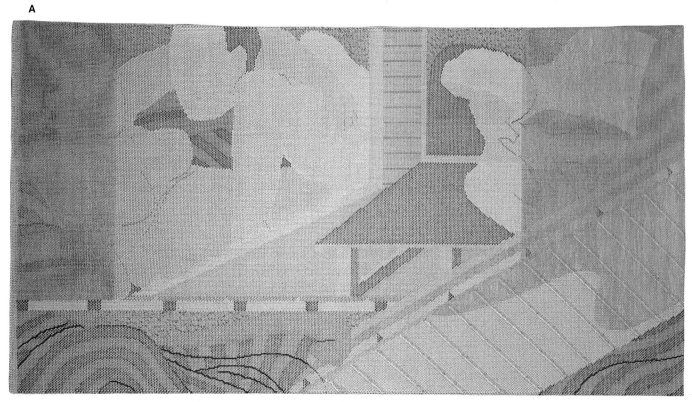

B

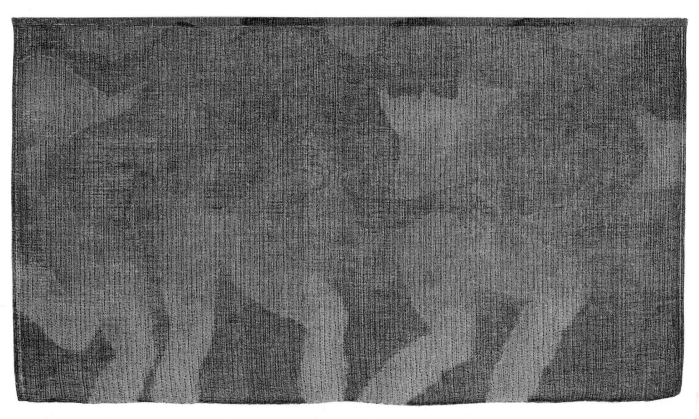

C

A
Cynthia Barbone
From the series, Amorous Games
Inlay, brocade, doubleweave; cotton, silk, rayon; 36 by 19 inches. Photo: Joseph Levy.

B
Sue A. Goudy
This One's For Twyla
Painted warp, broken twill; silk, cotton, rayon, acrylic, lurex; 82 by 45 inches. Photo: George Tarbay.

C
Betty Vera
Ashes
Space-dyed warp, plain weave with twill inlay; cotton, linen, silk, rayon; 45 by 34 inches. Photo: Veronica Saddler.

D
Sue A. Goudy
Twilight Rondo
Painted warp, broken twill; silk, cotton, rayon, acrylic, lurex; 396 by 54 inches.

D

A

B

C

D

E

A

Ellen Wood Quade
Cope's Fields

Painted warp, supplementary weft brocade; linen, wool, silk, cotton, rayon; 37 by 19 inches.

By manipulating the woven structure, the different levels of interaction combine and contrast to represent features of the landscape.

B

Kaija Tyni-Rautiainen
Winter Day

Weft-faced satin and plain weave; linen, lichen; 38 by 40 inches.

The inspiration for my tapestries comes from my experiences in nature.

C

Carol Lavine
Between Two Worlds

Doubleweave pick-up; cotton; 8 by 12 inches.

I try to capture a mood of place and time through the use of color gradation and the interplay of layers.

D

Jana Vander Lee
Sailing Thru

Theo Moorman tapestry weave, embroidery; linen, polyester, cotton, silk, wool, ramie; 4 by 3 feet. Photo: Frank Martin.

I had seen Raphael's cartoon for the tapestry The Miraculous Draught of Fishes *in the Vatican Collection. I was amazed at the transparency effect of the water. I wanted to express the volume of water and the feel of the breeze.*

E

Pirkko Karvonen
Grain Elevators

Multiharness inlay; linen; 84 by 194 cm (each panel).

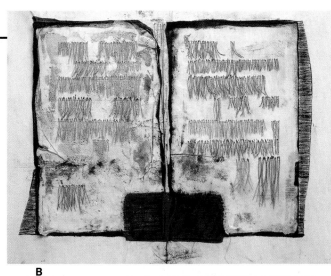

A

Sunhild Wollwage
A Note From the Wood
Batik, sewing; cotton, paper, cotton thread, pine needles; 88 by 74 cm.

B

Laura Foster Nicholson
The Orange Show
Twill brocade; wool, silk; 30 by 29 inches.

C

Patricia A. Killoran
City Sidewalk
Double painted warp, triple weave pick-up; cotton; 64 by 43 inches.

I enjoy the interactions of shape upon shape in architectural images.

D

Jeannie Kamins
Portrait of Gordon McGregor
Machine stitched fabric applique; 112 by 94 cm. Photo: Henri Robideau.

E

Deidre Scherer
For Grace
Fabric and thread; 17½ by 21 inches.

F

Deidre Scherer
Flower Bed
Fabric and thread; 32½ by 41½ inches.

I paint and draw with fabric and thread, using the techniques of cutting, piecing, layering, and machine stitching in non-traditional ways. With my fabric portrait series, I want to make honest images of the elderly.

B

C

D

E

F

A

B

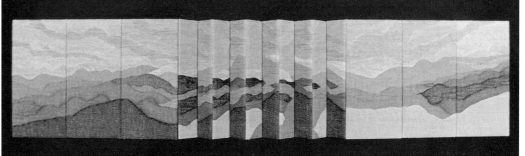

A

Joh Ricci

. . . of nature . . . of heaven and earth

Doubleweave pick-up, ikat; wool, bamboo; 21 by 58 inches. Photo: Amy Jones.

B

Barbara Grenell

Symbiosis

Balanced tapestry weave; hand-dyed linen, cotton, wool; 160 by 36 by 6 inches. Photo: Rob Grenell.

My tapestries are about movement and landscapes—of traveling through a scene, of clouds passing by, vision interrupted and fragmented by car windows.

C

Joan Harrell

Crosswords #4: Acid Rain

Warp ikat, complementary wefts, embroidery; mercerized cotton, procion dyes; 18 by 20½ inches.

D

Terri Hall

Fragment

Block weave; nylon, metallic yarn, sequin strips, silver card; 50 by 60 cm. Photo: Brett Martin.

Ancient Peruvian textile fragments inspired this piece. My interpretation uses 20th century materials, but attempts to retain some of the random quality of preserved fragments.

E

Sunhild Wollwage

Untitled

Batik; cotton, cotton threads; 90 by 94 cm.

F

Morgan Clifford

Cranbrook Calendar

Weft brocade; linen; 43 by 44 inches. Photo: Jerry Mathiason.

I want the viewer to be reminded more of a dish towel or tablecloth, and less of a painting. I use the "dish towel" as a canvas which is then overlaid with brocaded images, implying depth and space.

C

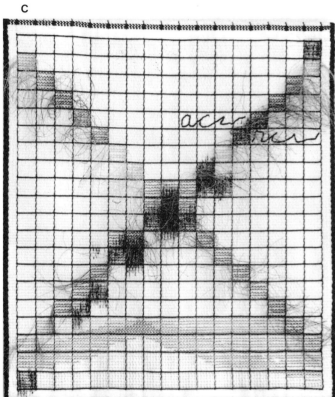

D

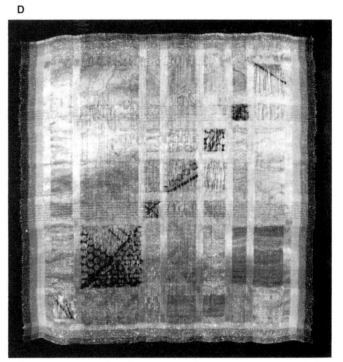

E

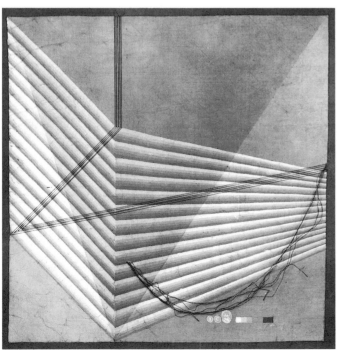

F

A
Susan Pauley
Sailboat Postcards
Dyeing, watercolor, stitching, collage; paper, fiber; 16 by 20 inches.

My artwork explores spatial illusions through ambiguous background and foreground relationships.

B
Donna Durbin
Taxi! Taxi!
Doubleweave pick-up; pearl cotton, painted wood frame; 23 by 60 by 1½ inches. Photo: Denise Watt.

C
Lore Lindenfeld
Japanese Diary
Fiber collage; Pellon, nylon netting, ribbon, lurex; 25 by 22 inches.

I search for those elements in the world around me that I can envision as fiber constructions.

D
Soui Yoon
Square, Squares
Rib weave, painted warp, interlocking; pearl cotton; 17½ by 18½ inches.

E
Janice Lessman-Moss
Green #1
Warp and weft face twills, pile weave, wrapping; linen, wooden rods, cotton, abaca; 24 by 38 inches.

A

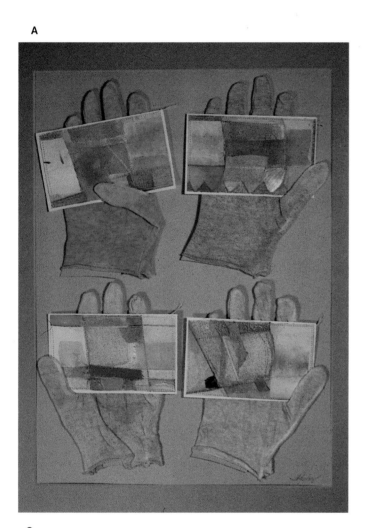

C

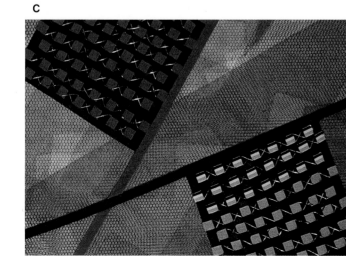

B

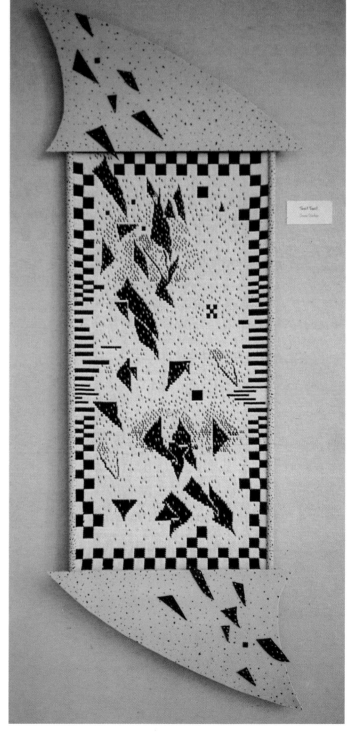

D

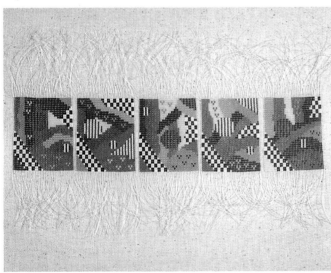

F
Betty Edwards
Untitled

Woven beadwork; glass beads, nylon thread; 14 by 11 inches, framed. Photo: Andrew Gillis.

G
Susie Cobbledick
Komo

Plain weave, knotted pile, stencil painting; manila rope, acrylic paint, linen, dowels; 292 by 96¾ by ⅜ inches. Photo: Kevin Olds.

E

F

G

A

B

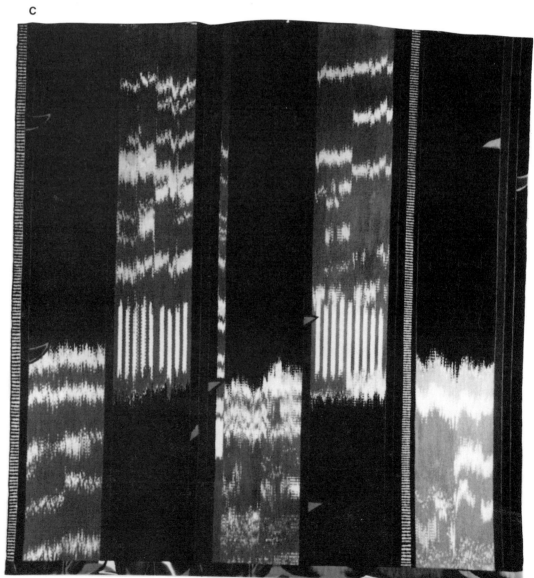

C

D

A

Robin E. Muller
Boxes: Blue

Twill weave strips, folded and sewn; wool; 7 by 5 feet. Photo: Julian Beveridge.

I weave long, narrow strips containing warp stripes of gradated color and value; these strips are folded and sewn to create compositions that are flat, but give the illusion of three dimensions.

B

Barbara Clemens
Zwischenraume

Patchwork, hand quilting; cotton; 23½ by 95½ inches.

C

Anneke Herrold
View Out Back

Ikat, strip woven, applique; wool, rayon, acid dyes; 68 by 82 inches. This work has a sense of freedom, but strong verticals seem to create barriers.

D

Josee Ebner
Wellen (Waves)

Wool, silk, metal, plastic; 100 by 240 by 25 cm.

E

Elizabeth A. Bard
The Wailing Women

Seminole patchwork, silk screen printing, beadwork, gold lame, polyester crepe; 15-inch waist, 30-inch hem, 40-inch length. Photo: Stephen P. Diers.

One of my favorite family photographs shows my great-grandmother, grandmother, mother, and me posing outside a big white Minnesota farmhouse. Although I was only about three years old at the time, all four of us "women" are wearing aprons.

E

A

Marla Gunderson
Raven's Hall
Warp face weave, stitchery,
painting; cotton, dye, canvas,
acrylic; 60 by 48 by 1 inches.
Photo: Ruyell Ho.

B

Barbara Schulman
Zig Zag Ziggurat
Woven tapestry; wool, linen;
101 by 51 inches. Photo: Mark
Wagner.

C

Jan Janeiro
Las Puertas III
Weaving, painting, patination;
raffia, paint, copper foil; 34 by
48 by 1½ inches. Photo: Dennis
Galloway.

D

Barbara Eckhardt
Through the Cellar
Interlocking supplementary
warps with weft inlay; ramie,
linen, cotton; 29 by 42 inches.

E

Anthony Tate
Duritti Columns
Glued, sewn, pressed, pleated;
dyed cloth, ribbon, metallic
threads, mylar; 48 by 81 inches.

F

Beatrice Schall
Nature's Shroud
Painting, sewing, wrapping,
burning; canvas, netting, silk
ribbons, reed; 54 by 60 by 1
inches. Photo: Stewart Schall.
*My work intends to invite the
viewer into my world through
the imagery; themes include
the rites of the passage of man,
such as birth and death, and
the cycles in nature.*

A

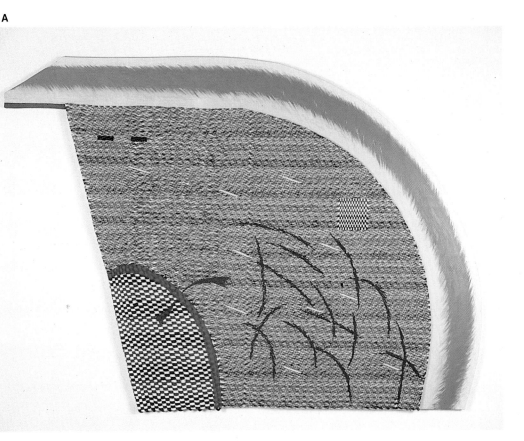

B

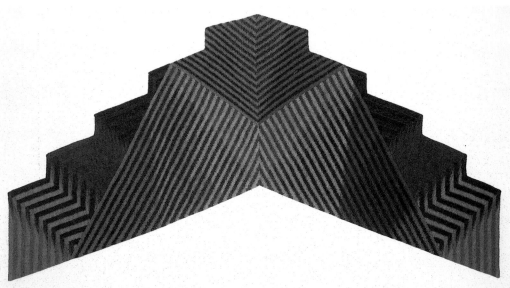

D

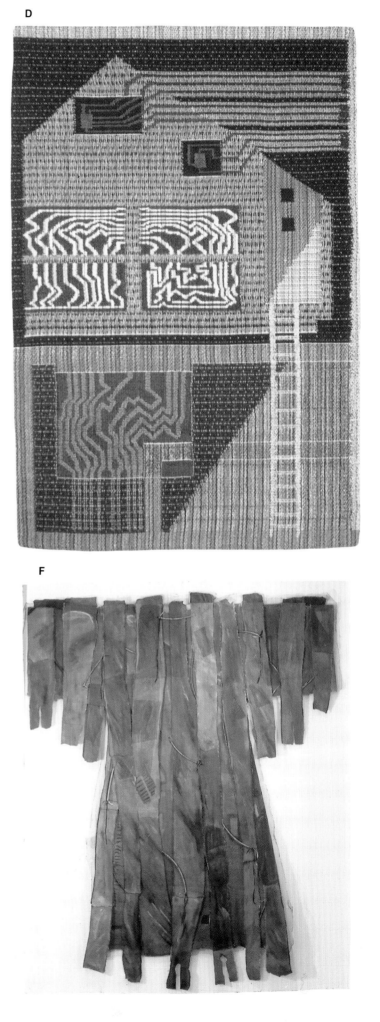

E

F

65

A

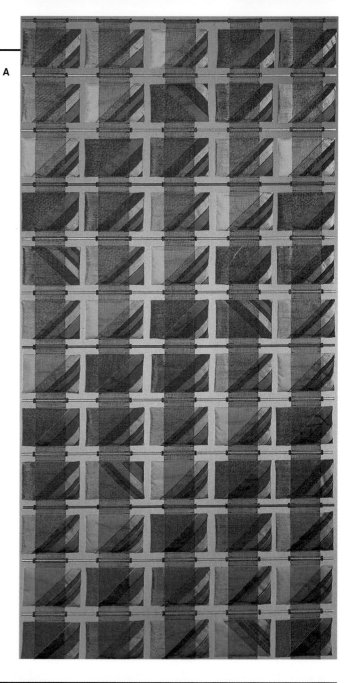

B

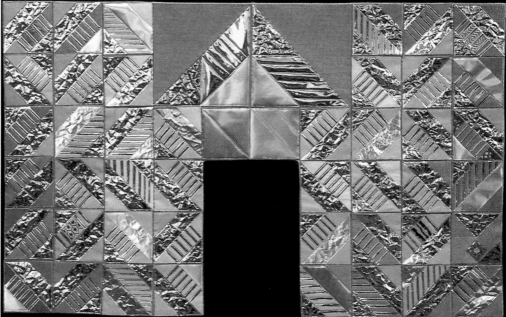

A

Judith Dingle
Maharani's Silks
Pieced, sewn, stuffed, painted; silks, wood, rubber, screen; 81 by 147 cm. Photo: Lesek Szurkowski.

B

Patricia Malarcher
Gateless Gate
Applique, painting; mylar, canvas; 60 by 36 inches.

C

Carole Sabiston
Spatial Possibilities: The Ruby Red Planet
Fabric assemblage, machine stitching; cotton, silk, metallics, synthetics; 10 by 8½ feet. Photo: Jeff Barber.
My inspiration: the dichotomy of order and chaos, translated to a textile language for public viewing by a random audience.

D

Mary Anne Jordan
Collected Pattern: Wheat and Hay
Silk screen, applique; assorted fabrics; 156 by 96 inches.
My work is inspired by historic textiles. I work to relate my fascination with historic fabrics in a contemporary statement.

C

D

A

Jennifer Moore
Triptych in E Major

Doubleweave pick-up; cotton;
58 by 44 inches. Photo: William
Dewey.

*Before I became a weaver, I
studied pipe organ and when I
first sat at a loom, I was struck
by the similarities between the
two—weaving harmonies with
colors rather than notes.*

B

Elizabeth Griffin
Earlier Strata

Woven tapestry, doubleweave
layering; cotton, linen, rag, bead
strands, telephone wire, sisal; 6
by 9 feet. Photo: Saltmarche.

C

Linda Hough
Phoenix

Painted warp, tapestry, inlay;
rayon, silk, cotton. Photo: Dah-
wen Kwang.

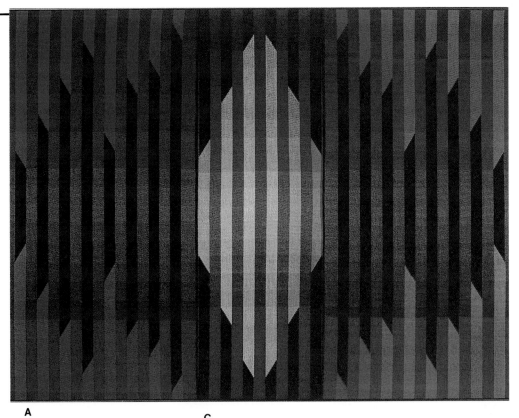

A

C

B

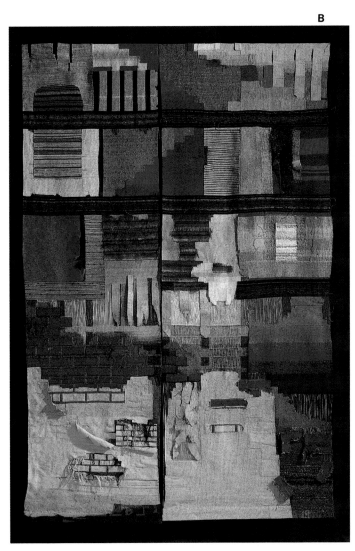

THREE DIMENSIONS

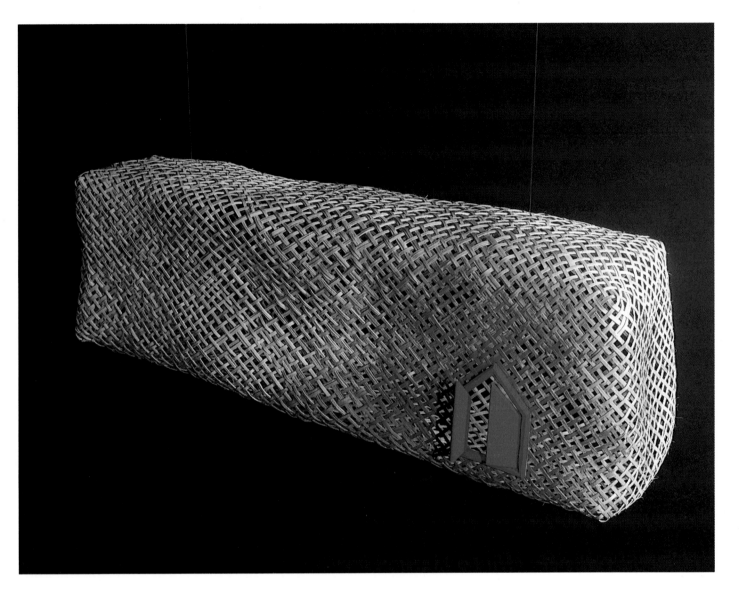

John L. Skau
Sanctuary
Plaiting; reed, wood, paint; 51
by 18 by 15 inches.

*Many cultures have devised
"soul catchers" for various
reasons. This vessel is one of a
series of temporary dwellings
for itinerant souls.*

A

Jean L. Kares

Elevator Dreams: Patterns of Harvest

Woven tapestry; linen, cotolin, wool, silk, polyester, brass tubes and rods; 7 by 29 by 7 inches.

The imagery is inspired by the Canadian prairies.

B

Pamela E. Becker

Lightning Glow

Painted, appliqued, and sewn fabric layers; poplin, ribbon, pearl cotton, textile paint; 48 by 48 by 6 inches.

C

Barbara MacLeod

Shadowjazz

Weaving, upholstery; wool, metallic yarns, assorted fabrics, wood, stuffing; 15 by 6 feet. Photo: Tony Wibley.

D

Pam Norman

Silken Staircase

Hand painted silk, Plexiglas; 6 by 14 feet.

My work explores illusion, movement, sculptural elements.

E

Donna Caryn Braverman

Rolm Telecommunications

Wrapping; linen, silk, wood, PVC, mirror Plexiglas; 9 by 14 by 3/4 feet. Photo: Julie Osterle.

Against a backdrop of contemporary architecture, my concern is to create fiber structures that will animate yet temper the typically severe lines of modern buildings.

F

Meredith Strauss

Modulation

Interlacing; cotton cord, metal; 14 by 5 by 1/3 feet. Photo: Myron Moskwa.

A

B

C

D

E

F

A

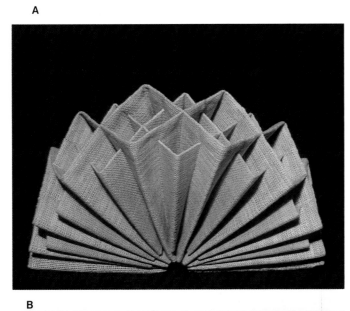

B

C

A
Paul R. O'Connor
Fan
Eight-layer weave; hand-dyed linen; 12 by 6 by 4 inches. Photo: Jay Magoffin.

B
Diane Burchard
Keeper of Curicancha
Hand-dyed paper and feathers, painted wood sticks and linen, encased in Plexiglas; 16 by 28 by 8 inches. Photo: Marcus Lopez.

As an object maker, I am influenced by the symbolic powers of ancient things and legends—fetishes, totems, textiles, even folk stories.

C
Barbara Bate
The Phoenix
Abaca and cattail fiber with corn husks, sea grass, porcupine quills, pheasant feathers; 10 by 16 by 8 inches. Photo: Rick Preston.

D
Steven Tucker
Impending Disaster
Assemblage; jute, boar's hair, wood; 12 by 6 by 4 inches. Photo: Michael Do'Bey.

My work is an intuitive exploration of the pyschological structures expressed by body hair.

E
Maureen Kelman
Untitled
Three-dimensional plaiting; nylon webbing; 52 by 17 by 5 inches.

A central issue in this series deals with the personification of opposing forces: movement and instability vs. solidity and weight.

E

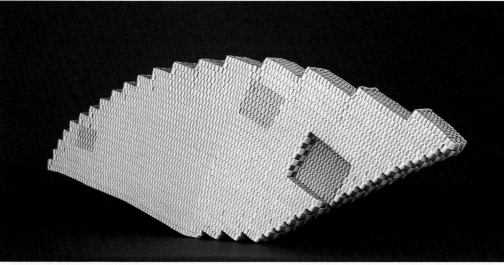

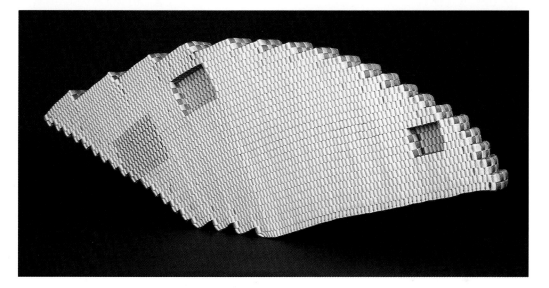

A

B

C

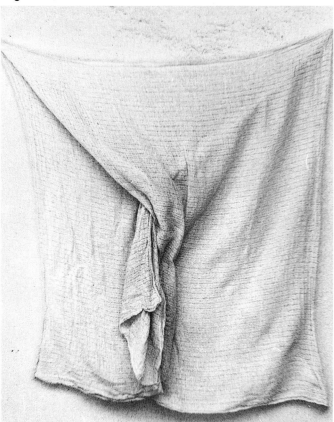

D

E

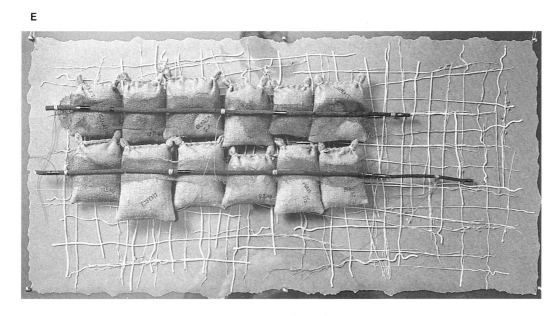

Rita Kriege

Untitled

Cotton napkins; 50 by 50 by 10 cm.

My textile objects are the results of forming and deforming, by stretching, drawing, pressing, and wringing. By these processes, the material takes the shape of wrappers of disappeared figures.

D

J. Michaels-Paque

Collapsing Rectangles

Gesso, cloth, fiberboard, paint; 132 by 12 by 41 inches. Photo: University of Wisconsin-Milwaukee Photographic Services.

E

Brenda Rolls

Bounty Bags

Millet stalks, linen, wire gauze, birch, copper wire; 84 by 52 cm.

F

Monika Duthie

Model for folding screen; shibori; silk, acid dyes; 88 by 37.5 cm. Photo: Edward Knapp.

A

Carol Eckert

Untitled Basket

Coiled cotton, metallic filament, wire; 3½ by 6 inches.

B

Florence Suerig

Tetrahedron

Folded, silver brushed, woven aluminum; 44 by 56 by 10 inches. Photo: La Bianca.

F

A

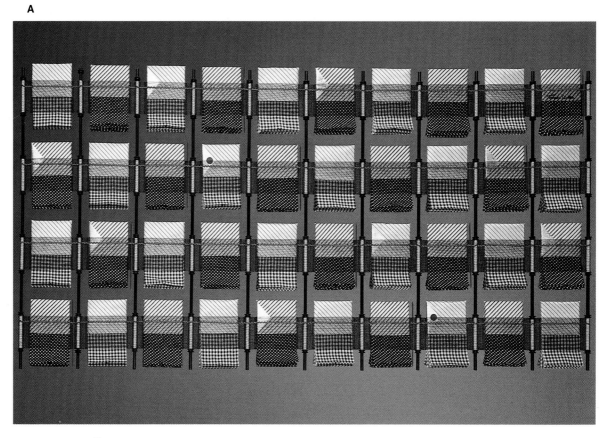

B

A
Judith Dingle
Origata
Sewn, painted, pleated, wrapped, beaded; silk, wood, rubber, screen, beads; 24 by 48 by 2 inches. Photo: Lesek Szurkowski.

B
Jan Ross-Manley
Installation, Ballarat Begonia Festival
Layered in four-banner units; nylon, scaffolding, dye; 6 by 4 meters.
This outdoor piece is designed to billow out in multicolored "petals" as the prevailing breeze catches from behind.

C
Lida Gordon
Untitled
Netting, painting; linen, acrylic; 24 by 18 by 5 inches.

D
Donna L. Lish
Swimming the Current
Hand and machine stitched, hand colored and magazine cutout fish; paper, metallic thread, vinyl, fish hooks; 30 by 28 by 2 inches.
This relief is the first concerning water flow. The rows of fish indicate the surface motion in a stream and direction of the current.

C

D

A

A

Joann Eckstut
Colored by Experience, #4

Knitting, assemblage; knitted cord, plaster, acrylic resin, tulle, paint, brick chips; 6½ by 7 by 4 feet. Photo: James Young

B

Dawn Macnutt
Kindred Spirits

Loom woven wire and sea grass; 6 feet high. Photo: Peter Barss.

C

Norma Minkowitz
Final Resting Place

Crochet, painting; fiber, acrylics; 12 by 9 by 12 inches. Photo: Bob Hanson.

D

Ilse Bolle
Occupied Space

Twined and tied rattan, bamboo, raffia; 30 by 34 by 30 inches. Photo: Andrea Mandel.

E

Denise Samuels
Cuckoo Cage

Tied and knotted round reed, waxed linen, paint; 20 by 20 by 52 inches. Photo: Kathy Luchs.

F

Suzanne Housley
Torso and Figure

Woven willow and wood vine branches; torso, 13 by 20 by 12 inches; figure, 13 by 23½ by 12 inches.

B

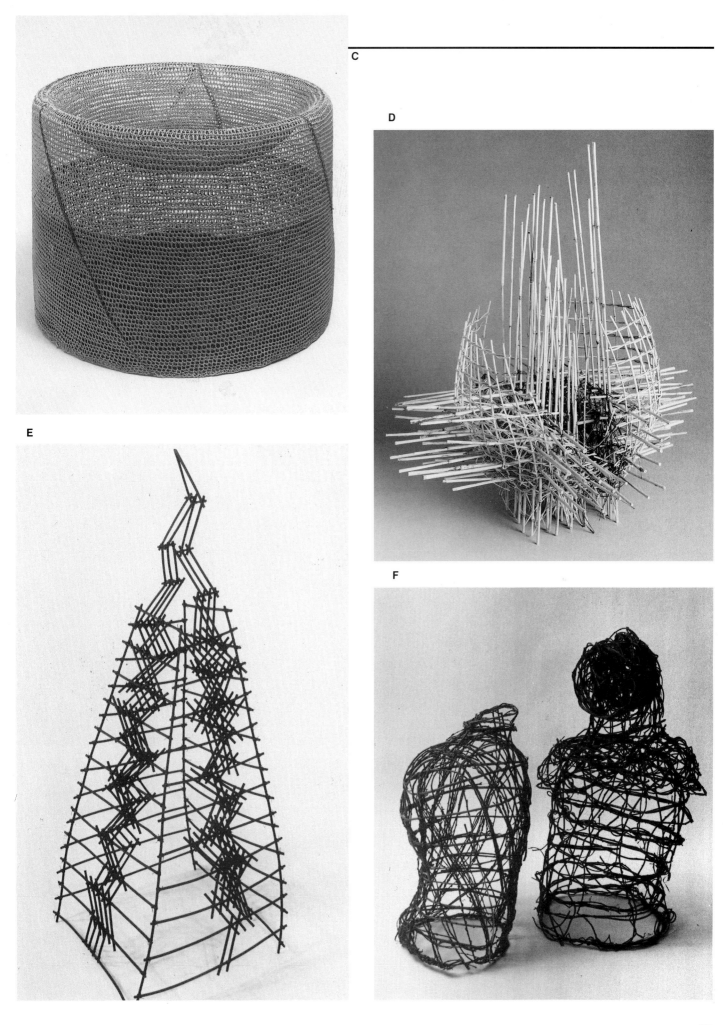

D

E

F

A

Robin S. Lewis
Changing Seasons
Bobbin lace; natural and manmade fiber over polyester core; 8 by 32 feet, each panel. Photo: Wendell Adams & Assoc.

B

Louise Jamet
Boite a Ouvrage #1: Broderie
Sewing, embroidery, wrapping, Xerox transfer; cotton, thread, colored pencils, bamboo, wood, color Xerox; 28 by 46 by 2 inches. Photo: Jacques Lavallee.

My work is a comment on the process and the tools used for sewing and embroidery.

C

Keiko Kobayashi
The Spiral of Bamboo Shoot
Peruvian scaffolding; washi paper thread; 70 by 80 by 50 cm.

B

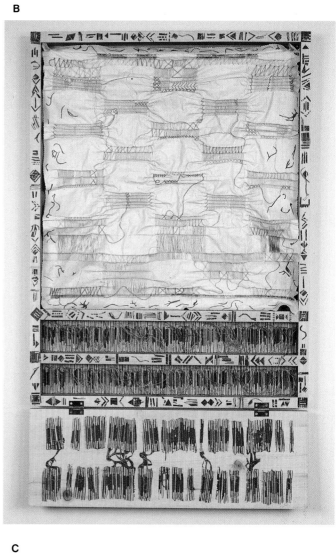

A

C

PAPER AND FELT

Beverly Moor
African Excavations
Painting, weaving, rolling;
handmade and painted papers,
metallics; 40 by 36 by 4 inches.
Photo: Jack Grossman.

*Time spent in primitive
countries, primarily Mexico and
Africa, has influenced my
thinking in terms of the
"archaeological landscape." I
first look at a landscape the
way it is today and then, as
photo images are
superimposed, I imagine what
might have happened in that
spot 50, 100, and 1,000 years
ago.*

A

A

Rebecca Ross
Pansies
Felted wool; 63 by 49 inches.
Photo: Carol Hassen Fisher.

B

Cindy K. Rogers
Meg, from the Paper Dog series
Pulled paper, hand sewing, applique; cotton rag pulp with lichen, glass beads, dog teeth, bass strings, gouache; 7 by 9 by 1 inches.

C

Ida Irene Guldhammer
Blue Composition
Dyed, torn, painted, lacquered handmade paper; 120 by 180 by 5 cm.

B

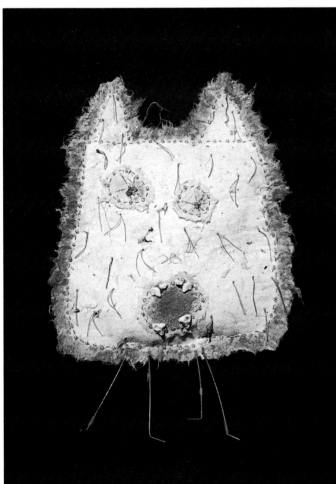

C

D

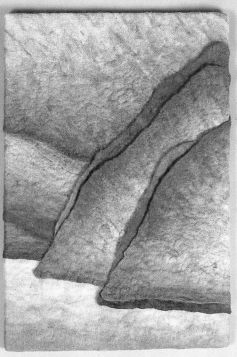

D

Marleah Drexler MacDougal
Rose Lagoon I
Feltmaking, hand sewing; wool, thread, fiberglass screening, wood; 32 by 47 by 1¼ inches.

E

Allison Doherty
Felted Drawing 18
Felt, paint, rhoplex, wood, cheesecloth; 52 by 34 inches.

F

Diane Shierry Meier
Proto-Byblic Tablet I
Felting, hand stitching; flax, cotton and metallic threads; 8½ by 12 inches. Photo: Sue Kalidonis.

E

F

A

B

D

C

E

F

A
Amy Grandt-Nielsen
Felt Fragments
Felting, natural and indigo dyeing; wool, cotton, silk, flax; 90 by 120 cm. Photo: Reklame fotograferne.

B
Leanne Weissler
Environment I Teepee
Poured pulp; gampi paper, bamboo, flax thread; 20 by 19 by 15 inches. Photo: Nick Saraco.

C
Victoria Brown
Yellow May Hat
Hand rolled felt, traditional millinery; wool; 40 by 40 cm. Photo: Henk Beukers.

D
Donna Guardino
Ceremonial Robe
Handmade paper, painting, assemblage; cotton linters, raffia, shells, feather, willow; 36 by 40 inches. Photo: Ron Zak.

E
Michele Tuegel
Southern Living Coat
Handmade paper; 48 by 36 inches.

F
Maria J. Stachowska
Wallhanging
Handmade felt; wool, silk, cotton, nylon; 163 by 100 by 20 cm. Photo: Edward B. Brandon.
A composition inspired by Polish folk dress.

A

Constance Miller
Garden Calypso

Handmade paper; cotton; 22 by 24 inches.

B

Antoinette Roy
Imbrication

Felted mohair, moulded plaster with dry and oil pastel; 41.5 by 21 by 27 cm. Photo: Yves Tessier.

The design and color pattern were inspired from imbricated orange peelings.

C

Nancy B. Prichard
Temples and Totems

Watercolor and handmade paper collage; 29 by 29 inches. Photo: Bruce Prichard.

In much of my work, I try to represent rhythms of daily life: night and day, the seasons, tides, cycles of the moon, work, etc.

D

Betz Salmont
Crecer

Molded and coiled paper; handmade paper, dyed raffia; 9 by 9 by 9 inches. Photo: Deborah Roundtree.

A

B

C

D

E
Mary Towner
Lickety Split
Dyed and felted wool fleece
and yarn; 85 by 39 by 1 inches.

F
Joan L. Kopchik
Pink Diamonds
Handmade paper, marbled
paper, metallic pigments,
thread, glass beads; 45 by 38
by 2½ inches, framed.
*This piece is based on a Log
Cabin quilt square.*

F

A

B

C

D

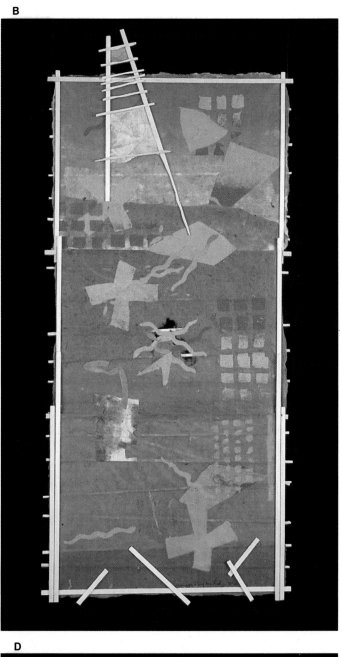

E

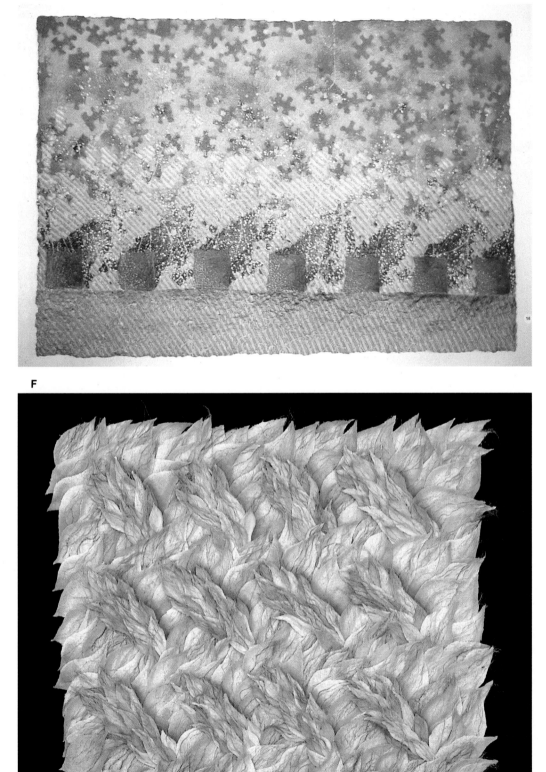

F

A

Hey Frey

Exit Above

Collage, stitching, painting; handmade paper, acrylic paint, cotton; 32 by 40 inches. Photo: John Guest.

B

Kathy Wosika

Hornpipe and Jig to a Reel

Wet pulp applique; abaca and cotton pulp, spruce sticks; 14 by 32 inches. Photo: E.Z. Smith.

C

Elizabeth Sibley

The Blue Heron

Dyed handmade paper; 31 by 44 inches, each. Photo: Alan Magayne-Roshak.

This piece is from a body of work investigating light. I have a fascination with windows, which as a direct source of light create unusual light/shadow shapes and color changes in interior spaces.

D

Yael Bentovim

Flight

Airbrushed handmade paper; cotton linter, shredded sisal; 55 by 50 inches. Photo: Claire Curran.

I love working in small modules which, when assembled together, compose large pieces. I love being able to play with the surface and to vary the texture.

E

Colleen Christie-Putnam

Untitled

Painted handmade paper; cotton linter, acrylics; 36 by 24 by 1½ inches.

F

Yael Bentovim

Controlled Blaze

Airbrushed handmade paper; cotton linter, shredded sisal; 55 by 50 inches.Photo: Claire Curran.

A

Carol Owen
Penland Night

Handmade paper, assemblage;
34 by 34 by 2 inches. Photo:
G.E. Owen.

*This piece is from a series
based on quilt designs.*

B

Monica Ellis
Untitled

Dyed, spun, woven, and felted
wool; 36 by 24 by ¾ inches.

C

Patricia Spark
Kazak Nocturne II

Felting, blocking, applique,
stitchery; wool; 32 by 35 by 1
inches. Photo: Dan Kvitka.

*One can blend the separate
colored fibers together and
then felt them; from a distance
the colors merge, like
pointillism.*

A

B

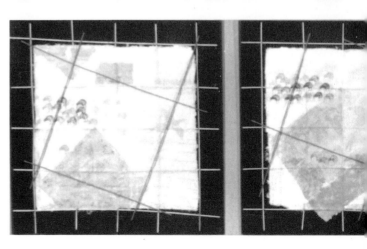

C

D

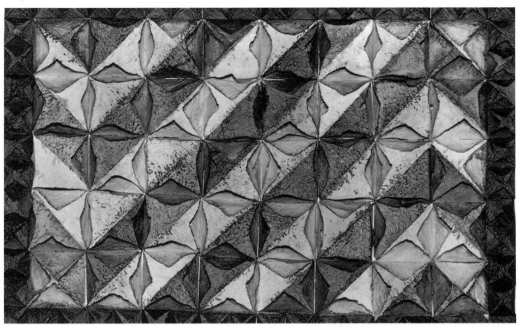

E

F

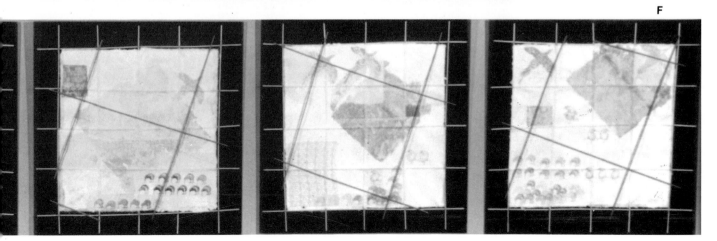

D

Carol Owen
Straight Furrows

Handmade paper, assemblage; 32 by 22 by 2 inches. Photo: G.E. Owen.

E

Margaret Ahrens Sahlstrand
Untitled I

Inlaid vacuum cast paper; cotton rag, retted Japanese mitsumata; 71 by 32 inches. Photo: James M. Sahlstrand.

I am interested in retaining the fluid motion and look of the wet fiber as it is being formed on the vacuum table in the finished work.

F

Sara Gilfert
Crossing Points: Charting the Boundless

Vacuum formed paper, wrapping, rubber stamping, block printing; abaca, kozo papers, laces, silk brocades, silk thread, bamboo; 167 by 31 inches. Photo: Brian Blauser.

A

Deborah L. Burton

Edges #1

Handmade paper, acrylic,
watercolor, dowels; 6 by 10
inches, each.

B

Barbara J. Allen

Yellow Stick Construction

Pleating, weaving, wrapping;
handmade flax and abaca
paper, linen, wood sticks, dye,
inks, pigments; 11 by 14 by 3
inches.

C

Charles Neely

Meditation, series #130

Handmade cotton paper and
dried grasses; 22½ by 33
inches.

*The focus of my work is on the
importance of line, form, color,
and texture as they constantly
relate to one another to evoke
the inner essence of being.*

A

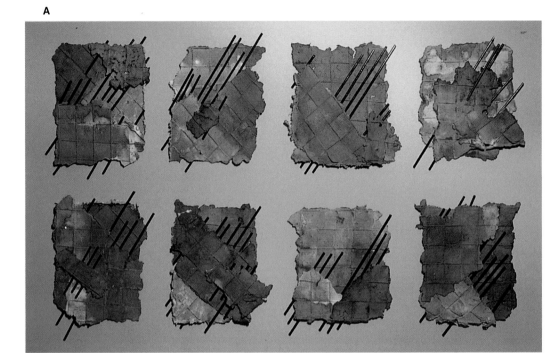

B

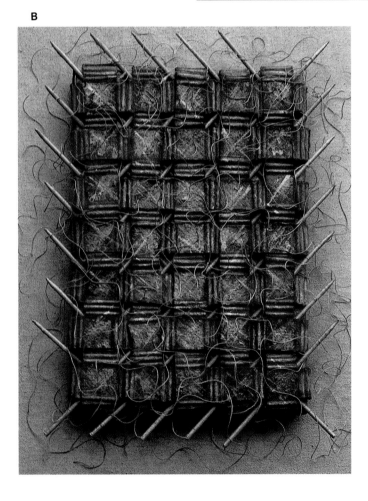

C

D

Denise Samuels

Stepping Out

Pieced, machine stitched, and
appliqued hand-dyed rice
paper; 36 by 36 inches. Photo:
Vicki Veenstra.

E

Renate Maak

Spuren (Traces)

Stamped paper with fibers; 110
by 110 cm.

F

Sharron Parker

Nights of Slow Dancing

Felted wool and miscellaneous
yarns; 41 by 48 by 1 inches.

*To me, this piece represents
the elegance and romance of
slow dancing, with its quiet
repetition of patterns.*

G

Roberta Fountain

Elementality / 10

Cut and assembled handmade
paper; 23 by 23 inches.

*The Elementality series uses
traditional quilt motifs as a
starting point for contemporary
design.*

D

E

F

G

A

Dennis E. Morris
Eastra II

Cast paper mosaic; cotton, linen, abaca; 25 by 30 by 4 inches. Photo: Photo Services.

I have always been fascinated by the tactile qualities found in the structure of crystals and geological formations. Using the raw materials of paper pulp, I fashion images based on the random patterns in those natural phenomena.

B

Susanne Clawson
Xinxim Por Cima #2

Handmade paper, abaca, cotton, pearlescent pigments, iridescent chips, silk and rayon threads; 32½ by 17½ inches.

Xinxim is a Brazilian word and was chosen because of the x's in it, which are in the piece as well.

C

Jann Rosen-Queralt
Halcyon II

Laminated paper over twined bamboo; cotton/linen handmade paper, bamboo, beads, thread; 30 by 40 by 5 inches.

My interest lies in gesture created by skeletal structure and stressed membranes. The forms are derived from observations of integrated systems present in dinosaur fragments, old sailing vessels, and architecture.

D

Maggie Holland
House Series I: Windows

Molded paper, embedded fibers; paper pulp, soil, straw, dye, plaster; 22 by 15 by 2 cm. Photo: Nancy Meli Walker.

I wanted to make paper works expressing and using natural materials incorporated in old Japanese houses.

A

B

D

C

E

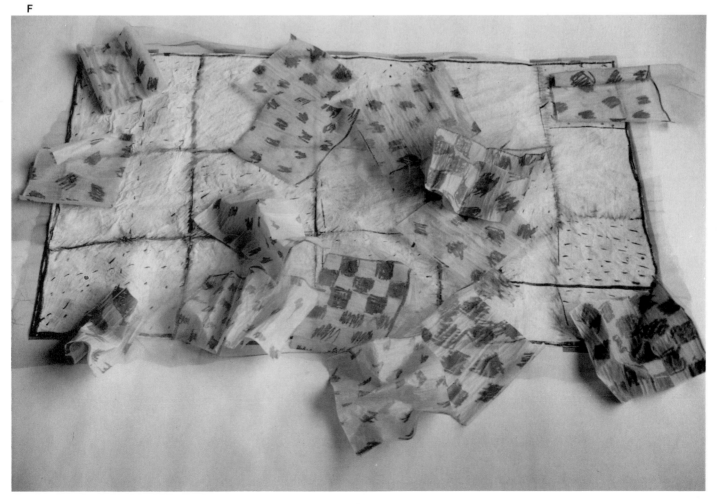

E

Carol M. Rosen
Intuitions and Boundaries IX
Paper and wood; 105 by 79 by
13 inches.Photo: D. James Dee.

F

Suellen Glashausser
Picnic
Paper, paint, netting, stitching,
wire; 8 feet by 6 feet by 12
inches. Photo: Bob Barrett.

F

A

A

Kathryn Maxwell
Trouble in Paradise
Handmade paper; 23 by 29
inches. Photo: Kathryn Maxwell

B

Carol Anne McComb
Silver Night
Linters; 30 by 44 inches.
*It is easy to be seduced by the
quiet reflection of a city at
night.*

C

Lois Dvorak
Life Among the Palms
Handmade paper, flax roving
raffia and palm leaf, ink; 25 by
32 inches. Photo: R. Dvorak.

B

C

BASKETRY

Zoe Morrow

Joint Accounts

Woven shredded U.S. currency; 10 by 9½ by 8 inches. Photo: Charles H. Jenkins III.

To me, my new woven pieces are two-fold. They are, in one sense, discarded paper recycled into baskets. Yet in another sense, they are totem vessels symbolizing the growing reverence toward monetary wealth and the fetish-like approach toward the dollar bill.

A
Dave Davis
Untitled
Coiling; Phoenix palm, waxed
linen; 32 by 25 by 20 inches.
Photo: Brent Brown.

B
Dianne Stanton
Conjunction
Plaiting; black ash, elm bark,
white oak, honeysuckle; 15 by
7½ by 15 inches. Photo: J.
David Congalton.

C
Audrey Mann
#1
Doublewoven round reed; 22
by 20½ by 21½ inches. Photo:
Roger Olney.

A

B

C

D

D

Judy Mulford
Evolve IA

Coiling; pine needles, clay, waxed linen, wax, dye; 14 by 14 by 5 inches.

I work with containers because they make me happy. Each piece I create becomes a container of conscious and unconscious thoughts and feelings: a nest, a womb, a secret, a surprise, or a giggle.

E

Judith Olney
Cosine

Plaiting; dyed reed; 13 by 8½ inches. Photo: Roger Olney.

E

A
Kathleen Moore Farling
Kiva Ceremonial Vessel

Coiling, personal technique; plastic coated wire; 9¼ by 3 by 9¼ inches.

Placing color can be like setting jewels.

B
Susan Sloane
Spiral #1

Twining; hand-dyed round reed; 16 by 16 inches. Photo: James Sloane.

C
Judith Olney
The Road Less Traveled By

Plaiting, surface embellishment; dyed reed; 12 by 12 inches. Photo: Roger Olney.

D
Nancy Goes
Happy Basket

Random weave; reed, acrylic paint; 12 by 13 inches.

E
Michael Davis
Key Note Bowl

Twining, stitching; round and flat reed, waxed linen, enamel and acrylic paint; 25 by 11 by 25 inches. Photo: Daryl Bunn.

A

B

C

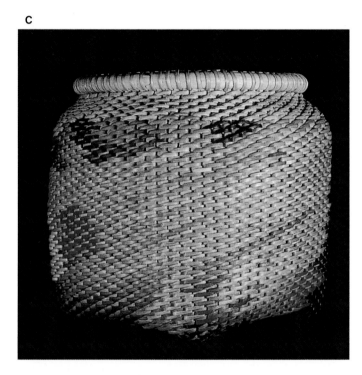

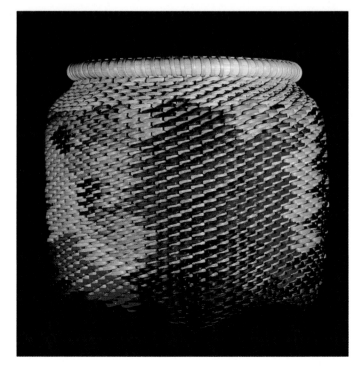

D

E

A

B

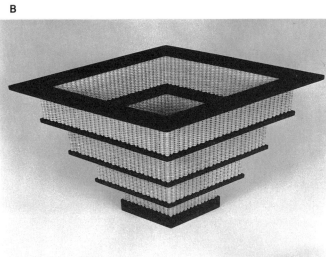

C

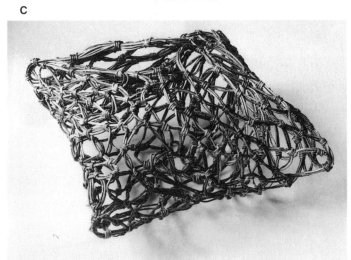

D

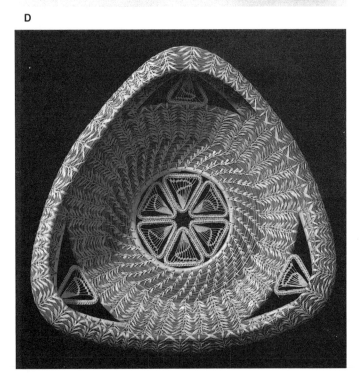

E

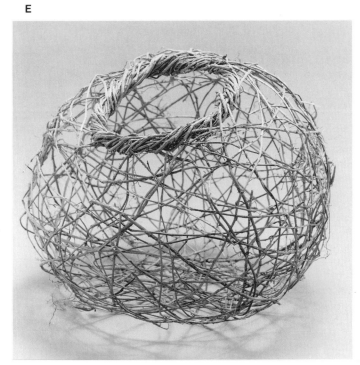

F

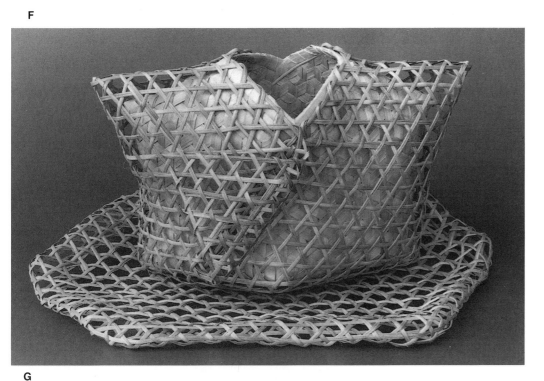

G

A

Dorothy Gill Barnes
Green Heron Basket
Complex plaiting; pine bark, British willow; 9 by 10 by 24 inches. Photo: Elaine Comer.

B

Priscilla Henderson
Diamond Bowl
Traditional weave, airbrushing, serial lacquering; rattan, birch, acrylics, lacquer; 22 by 11 by 13 inches. Photo: Lee W. Henderson.

C

Hisako Sekijima
Untitled
Wrapped and tied sinomenine vine; 11 by 5½ by 11 inches.
My recent concerns have been on the ways that objects are shaped or transformed from two-dimensional to three-dimensional, by actions of the hands such as bending, cutting, tying, or beating that are too simple and elemental to be named "a technique."

D

Marilyn Moore
Triangle II
Teneriffe embroidery, coiling; pine needles, raffia; 14 by 4½ by 14 inches. Photo: Ted Ward.

E

Virginia Kaiser
Free Form I
Free formed ivy. Photo: Roger Deckker.
I am a weaver set free through basketry.

F

Shereen LaPlantz
Untitled
Mad weave, hexagonal plaiting; lauhala, flat reed; 25 by 12 by 18 inches.
I like dressing, particularly in costumes; I also like dressing my baskets.

G

Priscilla Henderson
Pedestal Bowl
Traditional weave, airbrushing, serial lacquering; rattan, birch, acrylics, lacquer; 21 by 15 by 21 inches. Photo: Lee W. Henderson.

A

Michael Bailot

Perla's Song

Coiling; dyed date palm, inflorescens, broom corn, lichen, sisal, pepper grass; 14 by 9 inches. Photo: Mehosh Dziadzio.

B

Jamie Evrard

Basket 86.2

Twining; wire, fish line, plastic tubing; 24 by 24 by 24 inches. Photo: Barbara Cohen.

C

Patti Lechman

Voyage

Knotted nylon; 3 by 4 by 3 inches.

My forms are containers or enclosures for space, not intended to be used to carry and to store things.

D

Patti Lechman

Traveler

Knotted nylon; 3 by 3 by 2½ inches.

E

Char TerBeest

Untitled

Willow, driftwood; 10 by 15 by 12 inches.

F

Beverly Semmens

Aluminous VII

Loom woven linen, copper, steel; 21 by 16 by 7 inches.

G

Akiko Mio

Form of Knots

Knotted paper tape; 10 inches high, 4¾ inch diameter.

H

Rise Andersen Petersons

One Step Ahead

Natural and dyed rattan; 10 by 18 by 8 inches.

A

B

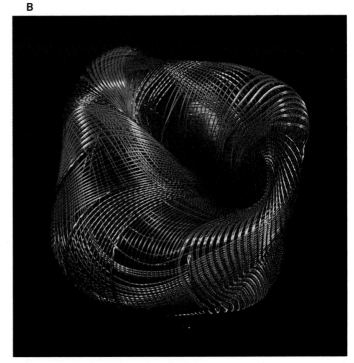

C

D

E

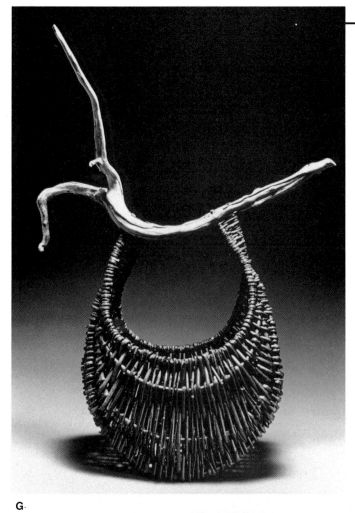

F

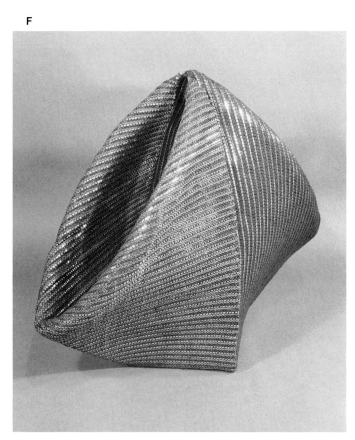

G.

H

A

B

C

D

A
Elaine Small
Celebration

Knotted waxed linen; 7½ inches high, 3 inch diameter. Photo: Wm. Small.

This piece represents fireworks that rush into the air, explode into colorful design, then descend as glowing embers.

B
Danielle Bodine
East Meets West

Dyed and bleached, plaited and woven flat splint and round reed; 10 by 14 inches.

C
Jeanie Eberhardt
Coils with Dogwood

Coiling; fiber rush, natural and synthetic yarns, dogwood twigs; 9¼ by 8 by 9¼ inches. Photo: Bob Barrett.

D
Audrey Simpson
Lilith's Pot

Jacaranda twigs, camel hair, black field grass; 6½ by 8 by 3 inches.

E
Dorothy Gill Barnes
Nova Scotia Basket

Plaited spruce bark; 15 by 18 by 10 inches. Photo: Elaine Comer.

F
Hisako Sekijima
Untitled

Randomly interlaced, cut, and joined wisteria vine; 17¾ by 14½ by 8 inches.

E

F

A

Shirley Halverson

#261 Cedar Bark with Pearl Buttons

Weaving, twining; cedar bark, pearl buttons; 10 by 10 by 5 inches.

I am inspired by the way native people take common objects and nature's products and assemble them into objects of beauty. I am touched by their thoughtful and restrained use of materials and refinement of design.

B

Jeanie Eberhardt

Coils with Grass

Coiling; fiber rush, natural and synthetic yarns; 10½ by 7 by 8¾ inches. Photo: Bob Barrett.

C

Carol S. Lasnier

Nantucket Lightship Nest of Baskets

Cane, cherry, ivory; 11 by 7 by 9, 9 by 6 by 7, 7 by 6 by 5 inches. Photo: David Egan.

D

Pat Bramhall

Native American

Sterling and fine silver, copper, leather; 2 by 2¾ by 1½ inches. Photo: Butch Bramhall.

E

William E. Pope

Nantucket Lightship Nest of Seven Oval Baskets

Ash ribs, rattan weavers, ash handles, cherry base, brass ears.

A

B

A

Dave Davis
Ceremonial Pot
Coiling, knotting; palm fiber, waxed linen, tamarisk, pine; 14 by 14 by 8 inches. Photo: Julie Bubar.

B

Rise Andersen Petersons
Winging It
Natural and dyed rattan; 23 by 17 by 15 inches.

A

B

QUILTING

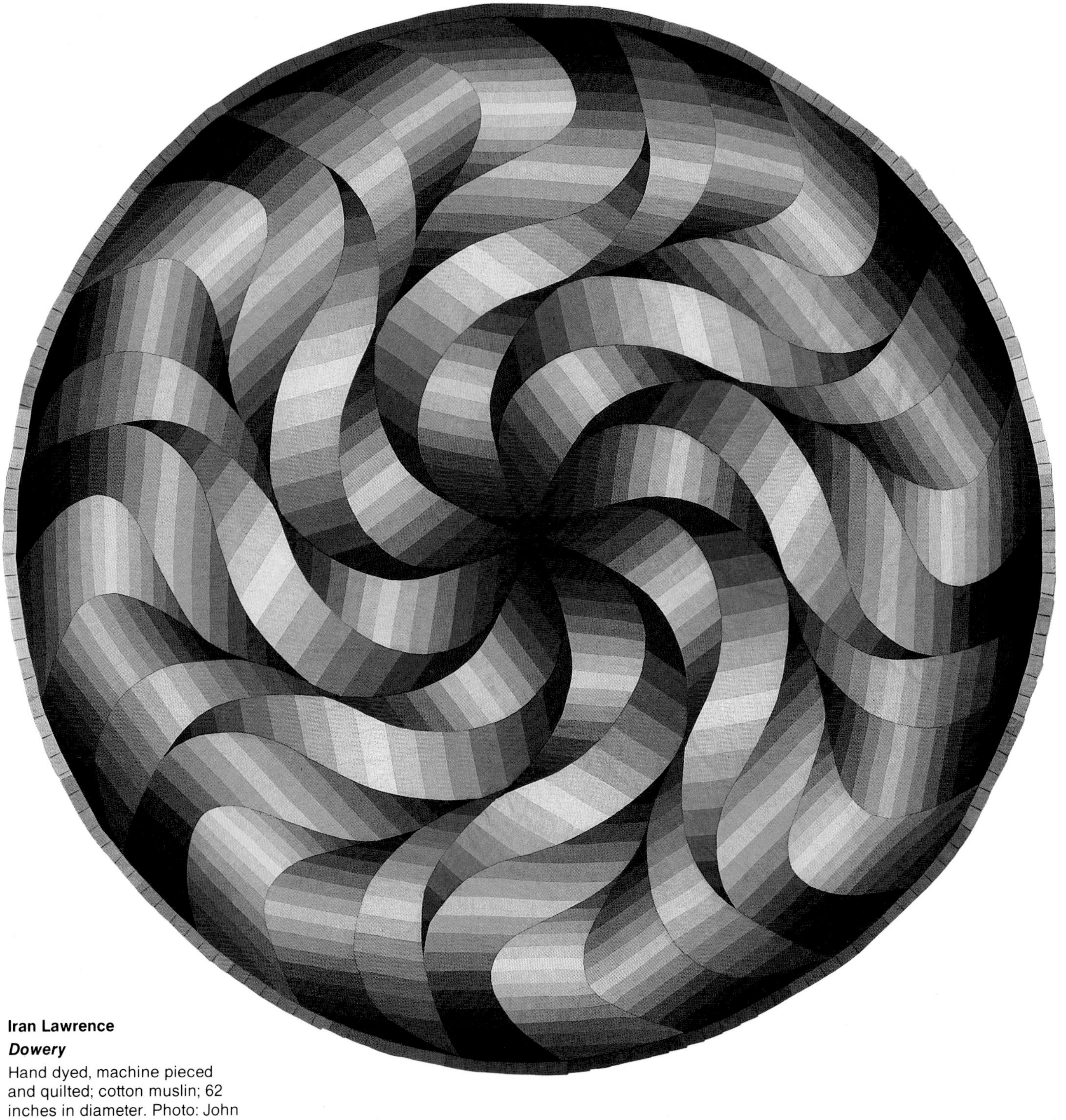

Iran Lawrence
Dowery
Hand dyed, machine pieced
and quilted; cotton muslin; 62
inches in diameter. Photo: John
Jenkins.

*I can draw upon a cornucopia
of textural and color effects to
bring visual excitement,
harmony, and warmth to
interiors of any environment.*

B

A

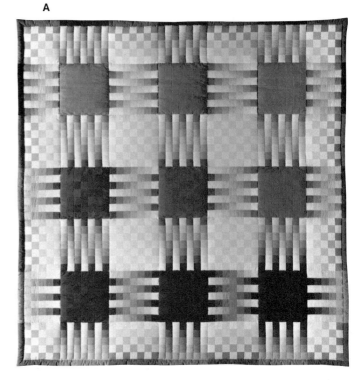

C

D

E

Suzanne Kjelland
Starry Night

Hand dyed and machine quilted cotton with embroidered signature; 60 by 60 inches. Photo: Ken Wagner.

This quilt was inspired by observatory photographs of galaxies and Vincent Van Gogh's night paintings.

B

Ann Johnston
Orange Peel

Hand painting, hand quilting; cotton; 20 by 27 inches. Photo: Jim Lomasson.

C

Ann M. Adams
Convoluted November

Machine pieced, hand quilted cotton; 48 by 48 inches.

I exposed the raw edges on part of this quilt for visual intrigue and then realized I also enjoyed the symbolism of revealing the other side and the honesty of having nothing to hide.

D

Bobby Lynn Maslen
Newport Jazz

Pieced, stretched, and framed cottons/blends; 42 by 46 inches. Photo: Robert Deering.

This piece is a nod to the first Newport Jazz Festival in the early 1950s. It is pieced in blacks, whites, and greys to give a feeling of musical notes, piano keys, tuxedos, and bow ties.

E

Joyce Marquess Carey
Reflections

Pieced satin, velveteen corduroy, and assorted other fabrics; 88 by 66 inches.

I have always enjoyed designing with equivocal space.

113

A
Jane Fawkes
Howe Sound Summer
Quilted and machine stitched cotton, painted with acrylic; 28 by 38 inches.

B
Vebjorg Hagene Thoe
Northern Lights
Machine seam application; silk, cotton, nylon, velvet; 39 by 29 cm.
Simple daily life objects fascinate me, such as beds and shoes.

C
M.A. Klein
Birds of a Feather
Applique, stitchery, hand quilting; cotton and cotton blends; 45 by 42 inches. Photo: Ken Rice.
I combine applique to give bright areas of color; stitchery to add dimension, texture, and pattern; and quilting to add rhythm and flow. This piece shows a fanciful scene around our bird feeders.

D
Lynnie Wonfor
Madame Lapin
Hand painted and machine quilted silk; 34 by 35 inches.
I've always enjoyed amusing myself by dressing cats and bunnies up in elegant clothes and surroundings.

E
H. Jeannette Shanks
Full Fathom Five
Hand painted and hand quilted silk; 68 by 45 inches. Photo: Judith Tinkl.
From the interior of the broken hull, I looked outward into a fascinating undersea world.

A

B

C

D

E

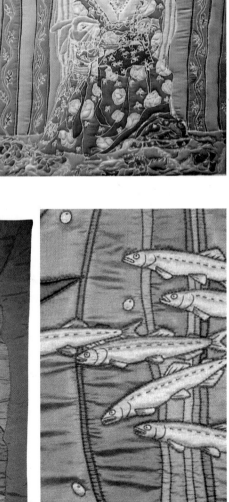

A

Dottie Moore

Home

Machine pieced, appliqued, and quilted, hand embroidered; cotton, cotton blends; 62 by 50 inches. Photo: Wayne Dyer.

This is an actual Greene County home near my farm. It is empty, but my imagination is activated when I pass it—I wonder who built it, who lived in it, why is it empty?

B

Betty E. Ives

Puttin' on the Ritz

Applique, machine piecing, hand quilting; velvet, lame, satin, cotton, blends, metallic threads, assorted embellishments; 88 by 52 inches.

C

Linda Gray

Lilac Storm

Machine applique, piecing, hand embroidery; silk, linen, cotton, synthetics; 3½ by 4 feet.

D

Nancy N. Erickson

Where'd the Savannah Go?

Machine quilted and painted velvet, satin, and cotton; 68 by 79 inches.

E

Judy Becker

Can't See the Trees For the Forest

Machine pieced, hand quilted taffeta and cotton; 63 by 64 inches. Photo: David Caras.

New England winters are long and I see these bare tree limbs from my studio window.

F

Jane Fawkes

Wedding Night

Quilted and machine stitched cotton, painted with acrylic; 72 by 72 inches.

A

B

C

D

E

F

A

B

C

D

F

A

Georgia M. Springer

Free to Go

Machine pieced, appliqued, quilted cotton; 51 by 51 inches.

This piece combines my interest in traditional quilting with childhood images of midwest farmland and the space and imagery therein.

B

Judy Hooworth

Double Homage IV

Machine pieced and hand quilted cottons; 180 by 180 cm.

C

Dominie Nash

New Day

Piecing, applique, machine quilting, drawing; cotton, dyes, pastel; 31 by 51½ inches. Photo: Edward Owen.

D

Clare Murray

Box Kites with Crayola Confetti

Machine piecing, hand applique and quilting; hand dyed cotton; 48 by 50 inches.

E

Judith Larzelere

T-5

Machine strip pieced and quilted cotton broadcloth; 96 by 104 inches. Photo: Bindas Studio.

T-5 is a color-field quilt. It represents space in a canyon where only a sliver of light can pierce the darkness.

F

Donna Albert

Red Diamond Series: The Poster

Pieced and hand quilted cotton; 32 by 36 inches. Photo: Jonathan Charles.

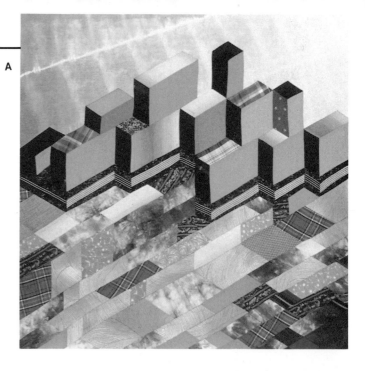

A

A

Carol Ann Wadley
River Condos

Machine pieced, hand appliqued and quilted cotton; 41 by 40 inches. Photo: Fred Wilson.

This piece was a challenge for me, as I'd never before worked without a traditional "squared" block and template.

B

Robin Schwalb
Let X = X

Machine pieced, hand quilted cottons and wools; 72 by 39 inches. Photo: Eeva-Inkeri.

This quilt is one of a series, begun in 1985, of "contained" crazy quilts—fractured squares within a well-defined grid.

C

Libby Lehman
Daydreams

Machine pieced and hand quilted cotton and cotton blends; 53 by 29½ inches.

D

Katy Gilmore
Boot of Paradise

Screen printed, machine pieced, and hand quilted cotton; 59 by 62 inches. Photo: Bob Shattuck.

I love the shape of these boots and love to transform their daily appearance.

E

Lucretia Romey
Provincetown Quilt

Hand sewn and hand quilted cotton and cotton blends; 43 by 52 inches.

F

Barbara L. Crane
Fall Field Day

Hand and machine piecing and quilting, hand applique; cottons, miniature animals, airplane, and other objects; 47½ by 63½ inches. Photo: David Caras.

The hand quilted lines in this piece represent the miniature objects' lines of motion or flight.

G

Barbara L. Crane
Out of Bounds

Machine piecing, machine and hand quilting; cottons, miniature mother-of-pearl birds; 50 by 59 inches. Photo: David Caras.

B

C

D

E

F

G

A
Janet Page-Kessler
Windmills of My Mind

Machine pieced and quilted cottons and cotton blends; 45 by 41 inches.

B
Valerie Hearder
Phoenix Vision

Curved strip patchwork, quilting; cotton; 38 by 58 inches. Photo: Ron Hrushowy.

Phoenix is a multi-racial community in Natal, South Africa, founded by Mahatma Gandhi as a peace settlement. In August 1985, Phoenix succumbed to racial violence and was sacked and burned. I made this piece during the incident.

A

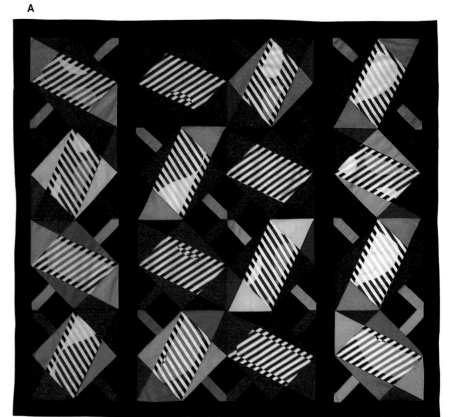

B

C

D

C
Judi Warren
Summerharp

Machine piecing, hand applique and quilting; screen printed and painted cotton; 54 by 69 inches.

My grandfather's sweet peas grew so prolifically that they had to be tied up with wires that were stretched taut like harp strings.

D
Clare Murray
Nightmare

Machine piecing, hand applique and quilting; cotton, cotton blends, velveteen, metallic; 61 by 61 inches.

E
Jan Taylor-Taskey
Red Alert

Machine pieced and hand quilted cotton; 36 by 36 inches. Photo: Jerry Prout.

F
Patty Bentley
Blue Study

Machine pieced, hand quilted and appliqued cotton; 48 by 48 inches. Photo: Ed Dull.

This piece is third in a series exploring a 3-dimensional look on a 2-dimensional surface.

E

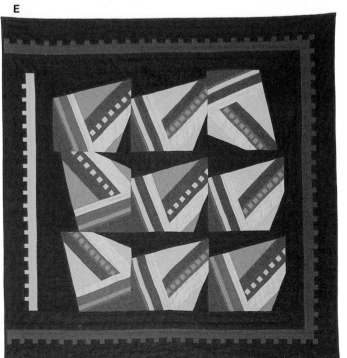

F

A

B

C

D

E

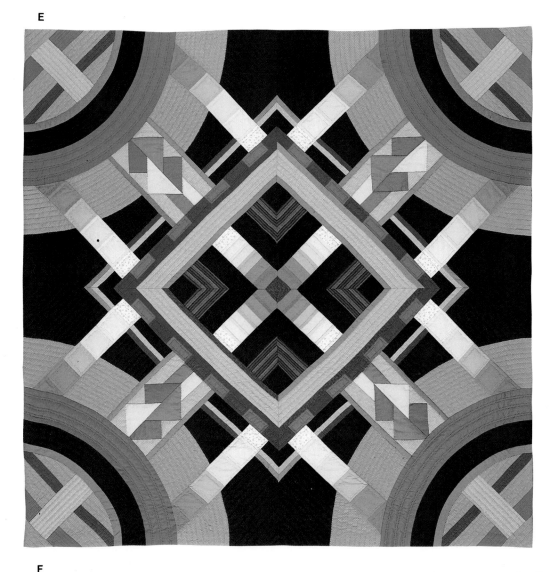

A

Judith A. Weiss
Merlin
Pieced and quilted cotton and cotton blends; 47¼ by 70¾ inches.
Paul Klee goes to Canterbury Cathedral in search of the Holy Grail.

B

Stephanie Santmyers
Risky Business
Machine piecing, hand quilting; cottons, cotton blends, rayon; 56 by 56 inches.

C

Marilyn McKenzie Chaffee
Crystal Medallion
Pieced and hand quilted cotton; 55 by 55 inches.

D

Stephanie Santmyers
Mixed Signals
Machine pieced and hand quilted cottons; 56 by 56 inches.

E

Judith A. Weiss
Bijou Dream
Pattern drifting, piecing, quilting; cotton, cotton blends; 49 by 49 inches. Photo: Calista Lawton.
This piece echoes the design of the art deco interiors of old movie theaters. I played bright colors against black to create the artificial depth and feeling of unreality that is sensed when leaving the dark theater to emerge into broad daylight.

F

Jane Reeves
Post Modern X
Machine pieced and hand quilted cotton muslin and chintz; 80 by 56 inches.

F

A

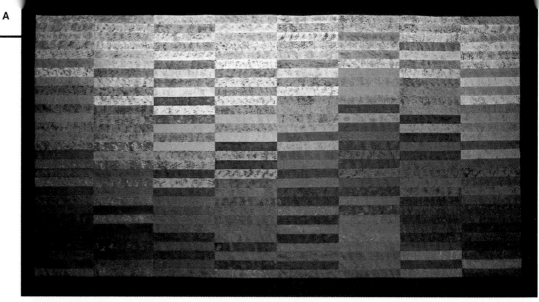

A

Emily Zopf

October

Pieced, quilted, and hand
painted cottons; 78 by 41
inches. Photo: Linda Kimura
Rees.

B

Judith Tinkl

Trellis

Pieced and quilted cotton and
synthetics; 74½ by 92 inches.
Photo: Saltmarche.

C

Lilo Kruse

Triangle Variation

Pieced and quilted hand dyed
cotton; 157 by 230 cm.

D

Judy Anne Walter

Larry's Day

Machine piecing, hand quilting;
cottons, blends, velvets; 48 by
48 inches. This quilt is #20 in a
series inspired by Islamic
patterns.

E

Lynne Sward

Unwearable Art II

Hand applique; cotton, cotton
blends; 21½ by 17½ inches.
Photo: Tamte/Wilson.

*Clothing as a design image and
the colored patterns it
produces continue to be a
source of creative fulfillment.*

F

Laura Elizabeth Green

Swimming Suits!

Applique, trapunto, quilting,
mixed media; swimsuit fabric,
plastic fish; 3 by 4 feet. Photo:
Mike Laurance.

*My affinity for fiber art is an
inheritance from the women in
my family who did intricate
handwork. In my favorite
pieces, the materials jump!*

B

C

D

F

E

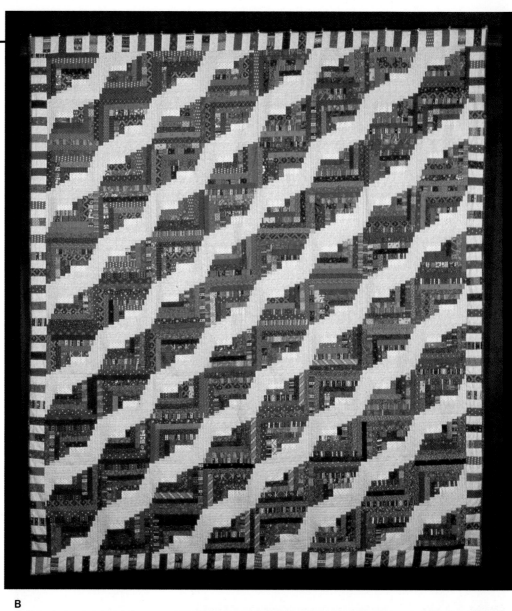

A

Ann Brauer

Color Study

Log Cabin variation; cotton; 90 by 100 inches. Photo: Tommy Elder.

B

Joyce Marqess Carey

Zinnias

Pieced satin, velveteen, corduroy, and assorted fabrics; 75 by 57 inches.

C

Erika G. Carter

Moonlight Matrices

Machine piecing, hand quilting, applique; cotton, cotton blends, yarn, metallic thread, beads; 41½ by 34 inches. Photo: Ken Wagner.

This third piece of my Matrices *series is meant to convey the sense of moonlight on snow.*

D

Jo-Ann Murray

Order and Chaos

Hand and machine pieced, hand quilted cotton and cotton blends; 62 by 62 inches. Photo: David Caras.

E

Sylvia H. Einstein

Charivari

Machine pieced and quilted cottons and cotton blends; 59 by 59 inches. Photo: David Caras.

This is the second of a series of quilts depicting the carnival in Basel, Switzerland. It shows the brightly costumed people milling in the streets.

F

Esther Parkhurst

Equatorial Currents

Machine pieced, machine and hand quilted cottons and blends; 13 by 5½ feet.

Each piece of fabric was put in place individually, much like a brush stroke.

C

D

E

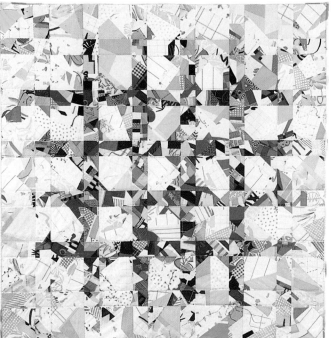

F

A

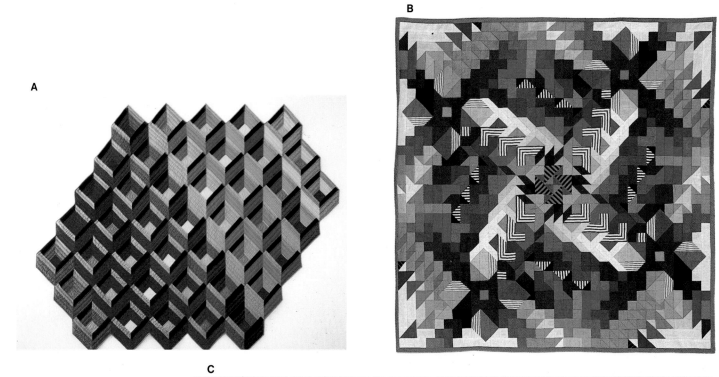

B

C

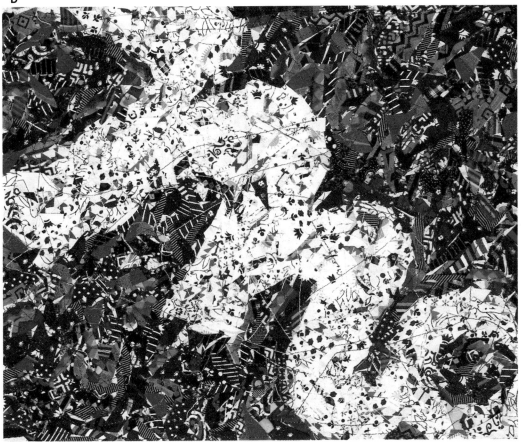

A

Patricia White

Little Boxes

Machine pieced and hand quilted cotton; 70 by 55 inches. Photo: Christopher Wafer.

B

Julie Berner

Universal Motion

Machine pieced cottons, hand quilted by Thekla Schnitker; 35 by 35 inches. Photo: Hugh Barton.

I am fascinated by pattern in nature and in the human environment.

C

Ursula Gerber-Senger

Metropolitan

Hand pieced and quilted silk, cotton, satin, and velveteen; 235 by 185 cm. Photo: T. Cugini, Zurich.

In textile design, I've realized the ideal combination of my love for architecture and my inclination to paint.

D

Lynne Sward

Fragment Series II

Machine sewn cotton and cotton blends; 15 by 12 by 2 inches. Photo: Brenda Wright.

The spontaneity of this "scatter and sew" technique is a joyful, unencumbered experience.

E

Judith Larzelere

Jappa Sunrise

Machine strip pieced and quilted cotton broadcloth and chintz; 113 by 84 inches. Photo: Bindas Studio.

I used many flecks of interrupted color to recreate the flicker of light on water.

A
Robin Morey
Athena
Machine pieced and quilted cotton and blends; 96 by 96 inches. Photo: Lee Rabideau.

A

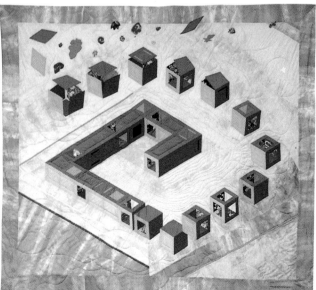

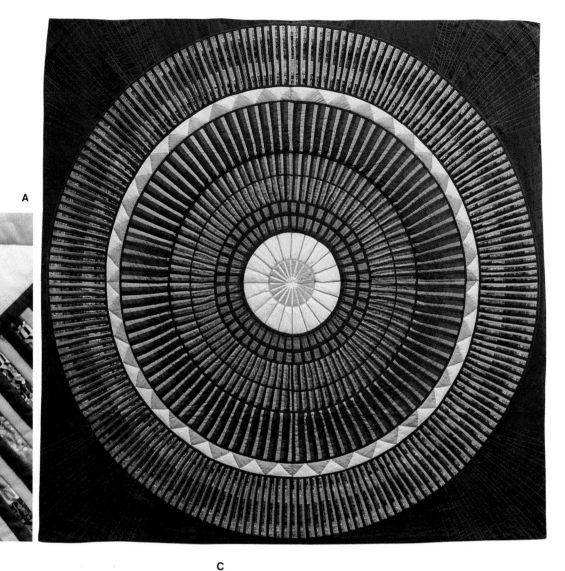

B

C

B
Barbara J. Mortenson
Breaking Loose

Machine piecing, hand applique and quilting; cotton, cotton blends; 75 by 85 inches.

I love the idea of breaking loose from any number of restrictions in one's life; with luck, wonderful things are released.

C
Pam Rajpal
Alegria

Machine piecing, applique, hand quilting; cottons, cotton blends, felt, gold thread, sequins; 27½ by 27½ inches. Photo: David Caras.

D
Faye Anderson
Spring Winds

Hand appliqued and quilted cotton; 76 by 87 inches.

E
Margaret J. Miller
Beyond the Bandbox

Machine pieced and hand quilted cottons and blends; 60 by 60 inches.

F
Anne de la Mauviniere Silva
Molinos de la Mancha

Macine pieced and hand quilted cotton; 60 by 60 inches. Photo: Michael Bowie.

E

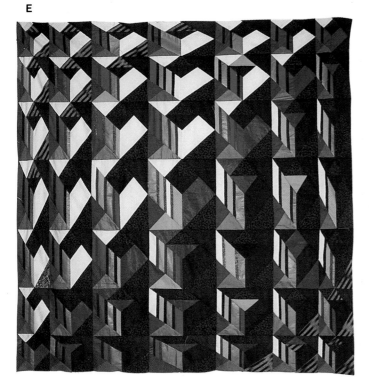

F

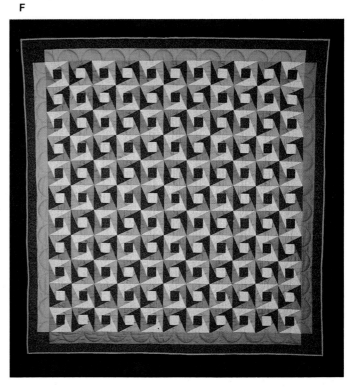

A
Nancy N. Erickson
The Clear and Present Danger
Painted and machine quilted velvet, satin, and cotton; 77 by 86 inches.

B
Vikki Berman Chenette
No Pasaran! (They Shall Not Pass)
Hand applique and reverse applique; cotton, mixed fabrics; 48 by 48 inches; design by Tom Spence.

C
Katherine Knauer
Streak O'Lightning II
Painted, machine pieced, hand appliqued, machine quilted and tied cotton; 77 by 70 inches. Photo: Schecter Lee.

This piece was inspired by the title of a traditional Amish quilt pattern which suggested to me any incident that takes only a moment to occur, but ends one's life or changes one's life forever.

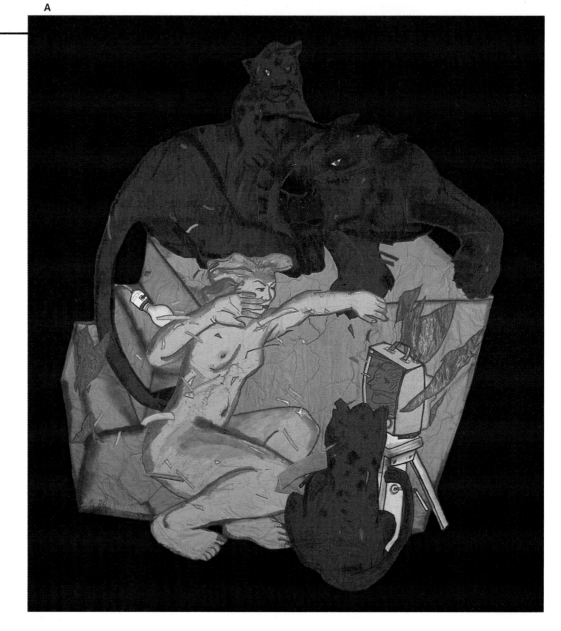

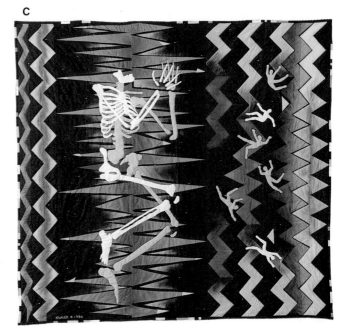

D

D

Katherine Knauer
Boys Will Be Boys

Hand drawn stencil printed on cotton, machine pieced, hand quilted; 79 by 70 inches. Photo: Schecter Lee.

Six scenes of warfare (prehistoric, Crusades, American Revolution, WWI, Vietnam, and present/future wars) are enclosed by rats awaiting the casualties on which they will feed. Climbing up each side is a strip depicting the common person who must shoulder the burdens of war.

E

Wendy Lewington
No Wife Of Mine Is Gonna Work

Machine applique and quilting; velvet, wool, cotton, cotton blend, silk; 34 by 46 inches.

F

Judy Wasserman Hearst
Out On An Indian Reservation: Seeking Help From the Spiritual

Photo Xerography, hand painting, hand quilting; cotton, beads, paint, feathers, leather; 48 by 50 inches. Photo: Ron Ricco.

This quilt was inspired by a song my grandmother sang to me.

E

F

135

A

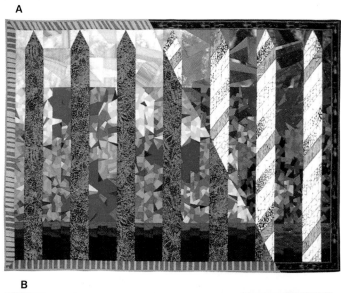

B

C

D

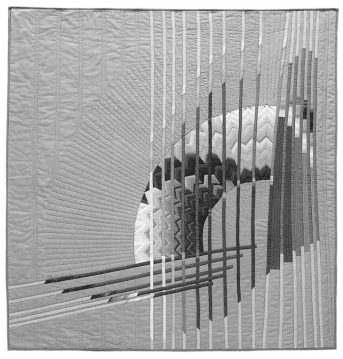

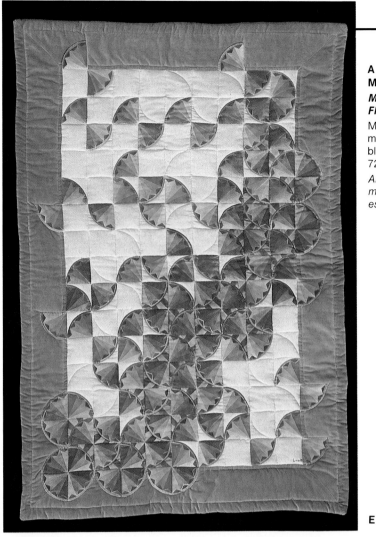

A
Marilyn Stothers
Mommy, Will There Always Be Flowers? (front and back)
Machine pieced, hand and machine quilted; cotton, cotton blends, metallic thread, beads; 72 by 52 inches.
An allegorical quilt expressing my concern about the future, especially for our children.

B
Nola Taylor and Marie McMahon
Trade Union Ceremonial Banner for Amalgamated Metal Worker's Union (front and back)
Screen printing, applique, embroidery; silk, satin, lame; 2¼ by 2½ meters, each. Photo: Oliver Strewe.
This banner will be used at Trade Union gatherings and will decorate the union's branch offices in Sydney, Australia. It depicts work processes and products of the metal trades industry. Research for the designs included visits to factories and workshops where A.M.W.U. members generously allowed themselves to be photographed at work.

C
Ellen Roberts Dreibelbis
Fan and Clouds
Painted and hand quilted pima cotton; 27 by 27 inches. Photo: Sharon Hudson.

D
Laura Munson Reinstatler
Fan Dance
Machine piecing, strip piecing, and quilting; cottons, cotton blends; 52 by 52½ inches. Photo: Ken Wagner.
I wanted the fan to appear to be undulating, suspended in space.

E
Linda Nelson Johnson
Stenciled Fans
Stenciled design, machine quilted; cotton velveteen; 33 by 48 inches.
This piece is based on the Victorian technique of theorem painting.

F
Martha Stilwell Young
Tai-Tai's Fan
Color Xerox transfer, machine piecing and quilting, hand quilting, embroidery, couching; muslin, cotton blends, floss, metallic thread, monofilament; 37½ by 31 inches. Photo: Laura Buck.

E

F

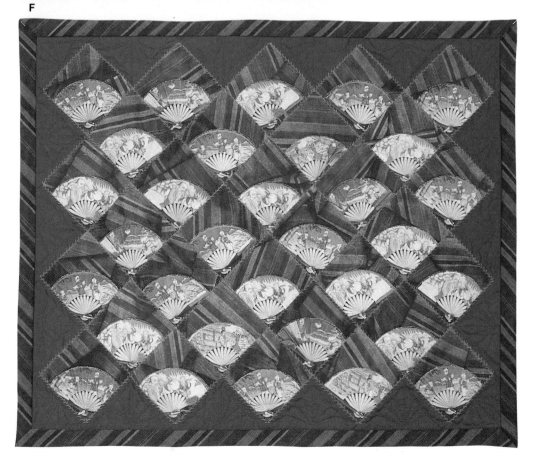

A
Faye Anderson
Volatile Material

Hand applique, reverse
applique, machine piecing,
hand quilting; cotton; 60 by 93
inches.

*An explosive release of color
and pattern.*

B
Sue H. Rodgers
Square Dance

Hand quilting trapunto; cotton,
cotton blends; 101 by 101
inches.

*The design for this bed quilt
grew out of a "doodle" on
graph paper, in which I played
with interlocking, overlapping
squares.*

A

B

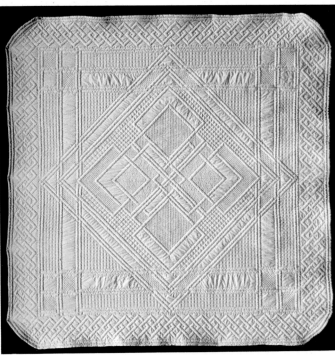

C

D

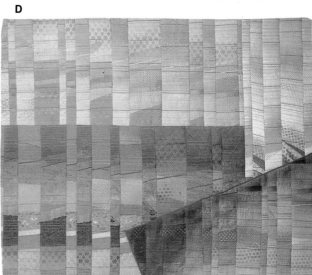

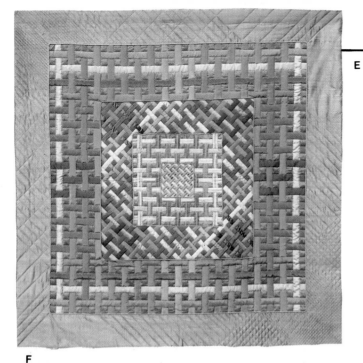

E

F

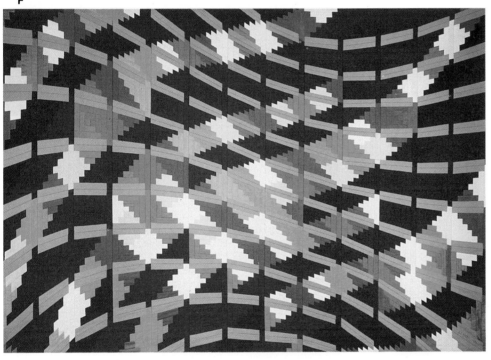

C

Jan Ross-Manley
Bunting Quilt

Printing, dyeing, machine embroidery and quilting, trapunto; cotton, satin; 220 by 212 cm.

A piece about Australia's Eureka flag, made in late 1983.

D

Ellen Kochansky
Prairie II

Machine quilted and embroidered assorted fabrics; 15 by 4 feet.

I am a collector and admirer of scraps. My current work deals in the blending of fragments.

E

Bridget Ingram-Bartholomaus
Untitled

Hand patchwork; machine quilting; silks, synthetics; 58 by 58 inches.

F

Barbara Macey
Metamorphosis of an Underground Landscape

Machine sewn log cabin patchwork; cotton, synthetics; 92 by 68 inches.

Each level represents a different stage in the evolution of a tiny part of the earth's crust.

D

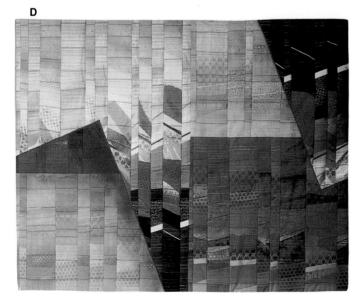

D

139

A

Jean Hewes

Circus

Quilting, machine piecing, applique; silks, cotton, rayon, synthetics; 102 by 88 inches.

B

Margot Strand Jensen

Outside My Window, Inside My Head

Seminole patchwork, machine piecing, hand applique, free form machine quilting with metallic thread; 47 by 56½ inches.

This piece revolves around the concepts of "Art imitates life," reality versus fantasy, and what is in one's mind as well as what is in the minds of others.

A

B

SURFACE DESIGN

Marty Noble
Knee Deep in Bloom
Wax resist and painting with
fabric dyes on silk broadcloth;
18 by 24 inches. Photo: Hallas
Color Lab.

A

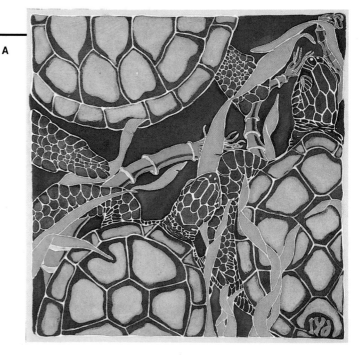

B

C

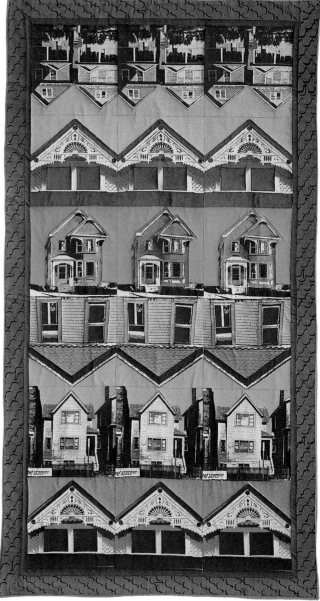

D

E

F

G

A

Helen Suits

Sea Turtles

Trapunto, batik, hand stitching; muslin, Procion dyes, embroidery thread; 60 by 60 by 3 inches.

B

Lauren Gregersen-Brow

Scarf

Wax resist and hand painting with Procion dyes on silk chiffon; 44 by 46 inches.

C

Louise Slobodan

Strathcona Streets

Photo silkscreen, hand painting, and machine quilting on muslin; 27 by 51 inches. Photo: Tony Redpath.

This piece was designed for a special exhibition celebrating Vancouver's Centennial in 1986. The buildings depicted are from Strathcona, one of the older parts of the city.

D

Roxana Bartlett

Return / The Dreams that Wolf-Dog Told Me

Piecing, applique, painting, printing, quilting; cotton, acetate satin, fabric paint, printing ink; 54 by 54 inches.

The landscape of my quilts is not real, but transformed by emotion into one which is distilled and evocative as in a memory of long ago or a dream. The Wolf-Dog series draws from the spirit of fairy tales and myths in which humans and animals can take each other's shapes and identities.

E

Sandra Kessler

Lilly Mountain

Procion dyes and resist on silk taffeta; 48 by 35 inches.

F

Louise Slobodan

Island Forest

Photo silk screen and machine quilting on muslin; 13 by 4 by 1 inches. Photo: Tony Redpath.

G

Liese Bronfenbrenner

1928 Birthday Party

Kwik-Print dye photo prints, painting, hand and machine embroidery and quilting, applique; cotton, cotton / polyester; 37 by 31½ inches.

A

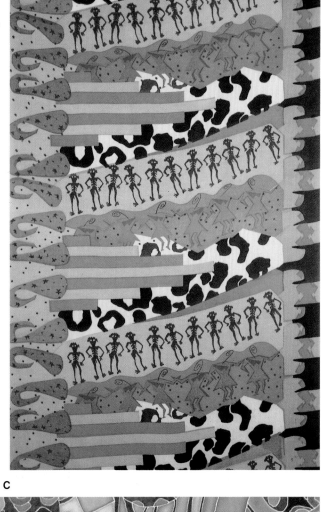

B

C

D

E

F

A
Sarah Quinton
Eclectic Boogie
Silk screen on rayon yardage; 36 by 108 inches.

B
Jennifer Bradley
Untitled
Silk screened and airbrushed silk yardage. Photo: Danielle Broomham.
These fabrics have been based on water and the life therein. I found that the qualities of these images (flow and movement) correspond to those of fabric.

C
Carolyn A. Dahl
From the Sky Series
Hand painting on silk; 46 by 82 inches.
The door to outer space is the sky—always above us, always unknown, and always a source of creative imaginings.

D
Gloria Kim
Triangles in Chaos
Hand painting on cotton twill; 36 by 90 inches. Photo: Tony Wessling.

E
Lis Jensen
New York
Monoprinting and direct application on silk broadcloth; 47 by 36 inches.
I think of my fabrics as "mood pieces." Here, I associate the light colors, gold, and metallic blue with the sophistication of a metropolis like New York.

F
Monika Duthie
Untitled
Silk screen on cotton yardage. Photo: Edward Knapp.

A

Doreen Lah

The Explorer

Stamped metallic paints on cotton, oil pastels, painted wood frame; 26 by 24 inches.

B

Marty Noble

Water Maidens

Wax resist and painting on silk broadcloth; 16 by 28 inches. Photo: Hallas Color Lab.

C

Beryl Stutchbury

The Amphitheatre

Silk screened and airbrushed gabardine; 100 by 135 cm. Photo: John Stutchbury.

I am inspired by the light and atmosphere of the varied Australian scenery.

D

Tery Pellettier

Sails / Planet Waves

Hand painting on silk; 36 by 65 inches.

E

Janice Anthony

Antipodes

Painted, machine pieced, and hand quilted cotton; 30 by 42 inches.

F

Tim Brooks

Rockets

Wax resist and painting on cotton broadcloth; 15 by 16 inches. Photo: Judith Wardwell.

I have been working with batik since I was 5. Now I am 12. A couple of years ago, my mother showed me how to paint the dye. That's more fun.

G

Leslie Rogers

Tossed Flowers

Gutta serti resist and direct application on silk crepe de chine; 34 by 34 inches.

A

C

B

D

E

F

G

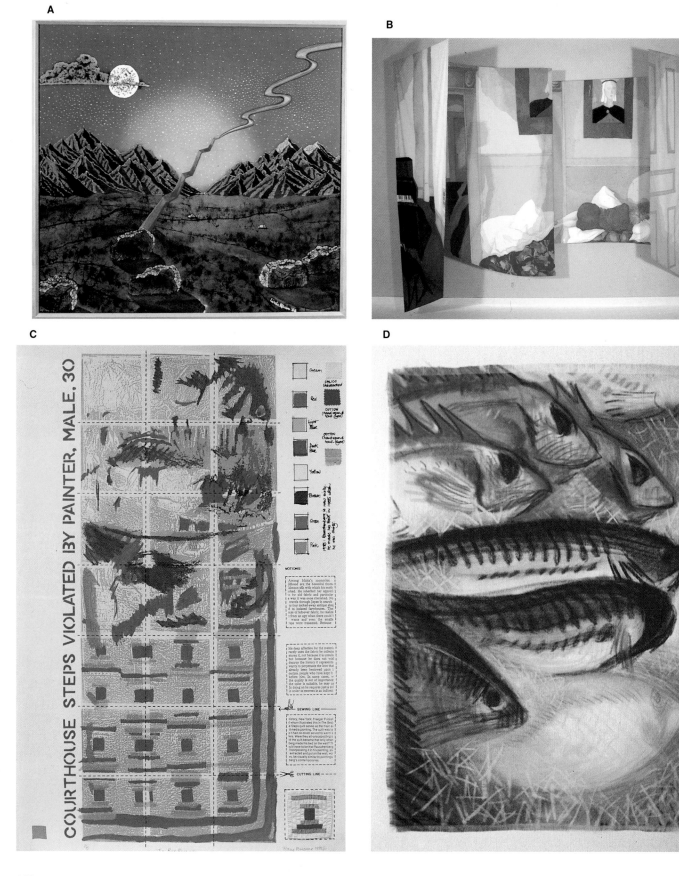

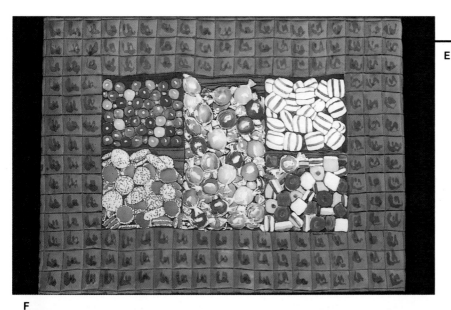

E

F

G

A

Linda Kaun

Once We Did Run

Batik and embroidery on cotton; 33 by 30 by 1½ inches.

B

Susan M. Moran

Ava

Silk screen and painting on cotton; 106 by 86 by 36 inches.

This piece is meant to be a portrait, by way of a series of viewpoints of the person in an intimate domestic environment.

C

Mary Newsome

The Bed Re-Made

Silk screen, patchwork, quilting; handspun cotton, calico, paper, thread; 84 by 122 cm.

I admire Robert Rauschenberg's work immensely but when I first saw The Bed, *with its patchwork quilt dripped and spattered with paint, I was outraged. It seemed to me the epitome of the disregard for and downgrading of folk art. I thought I would set things right and re-make Rauschenberg's bed . . .*

D

Jane Marshall-Wild

St. Clair Market #2

Drawing and painting on silk; 32 by 26 cm.

The image comes from the local fish market.

E

Marilyn Lawrance Harrison

Candy Quilt I

Wax resist, direct dye, machine quilting; viscose satin; 39 by 28 inches.

My Candy Quilts were inspired by the Mast Store and Annex in North Carolina, where old-fashioned candies are displayed like crown jewels.

F

Judy L. Kahle

Atmospheric Forecast

Direct dye application with gutta resist on china silk; 78 by 45 inches.

G

Linda Elsa Perala

Brazilian Dancers

Subtraction with bleach, batik, handcoloring; black viscose rayon; 45 by 36 inches.

A

Christine Schechter

Three-Three

Doubleweave, space dyeing;
linen; 31 by 31 inches.

B

Laura Militzer Bryant

Reflecting Pool

Doubleweave with broken twill,
space dyeing; wool; 107 by 48
inches. Photo: Phototech.

*This piece explores the
evocation of landscapes / city
scapes and uses the crispness
of doublewoven squares to
contrast with the "reflection" of
dyed images.*

C

Susan Atwell

Dress Blues

Ikat and inlay; cotton; 27 by 27
inches.

*This image is of my
grandparents when they were
newly married. It's also one of
my favorites because I now
wear the shirt my grandfather is
wearing in the photograph.*

D

Mary Rawcliffe Colton

Ikat Rotation

Warp ikat, surface
embellishment; cotton, rayon,
silk, linen; 53 by 54 inches.
Photo: Carla Breeze.

*Much of the fun of ikat comes
from surprises. Although one
carefully plans and prepares a
warp, colors may blend in the
dyeing and threads may slip
when being wound on a loom.
This piece begged for further
play—cutting, rearranging, and
embellishing.*

E

Joan Hausrath

Rhythms at Dusk

Dip dyeing, ikat, handweaving;
wool; 58 by 60 inches.

*From a formal standpoint, I play
with the visual effects and
dynamic placements of color.
Yet my aim is that each piece
reveal a spirit that goes beyond
analysis.*

F

Marilyn Beal

City Rain

Warp and weft painting,
irregular twill; cotton, linen, silk;
20 by 29 inches.

A

B

C

D

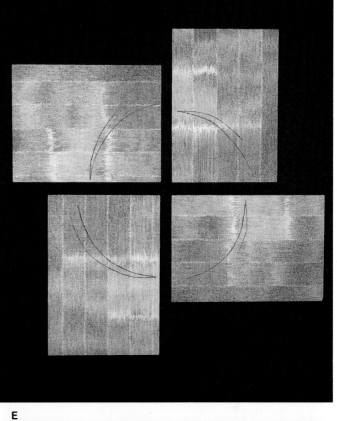

E

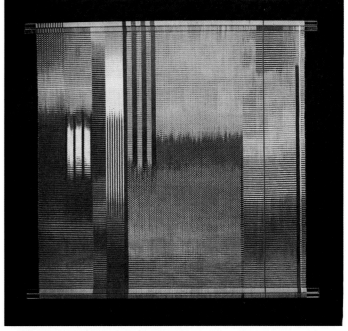

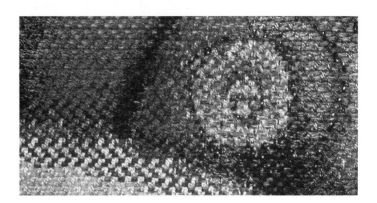

F

A

A

Robin Pyzik-Shuler
Shibori Flag I
Arashi shibori on cotton; 64 by 48 inches.

B

Erica Licea-Kane
Private Thoughts #4
Shibori, assemblage, machine sewing; cotton, spray paint; 42 by 42 inches. Photo: Carole Starz.

The visual references in my work are derived from aerial views, maps, and the landscape. My intentions are to create absorbing and sensual surfaces that can be explored and changed, depending on the viewer's distance.

C

Lesley Richmond
Skies of Saturn #2
Assemblage, pleating, layer dyeing; silk organdy, Plexiglas, nails; 22 by 28 by 1½ inches.

D

Lucy A. Jahns
Changes
Dyeing, drawing, machine applique and embroidery; cotton, colored pencil, thread; 37 by 37 inches.

In this piece, I used my love for pattern and color to create a surface rich in decoration.

B

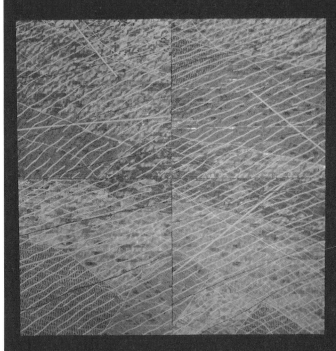

C

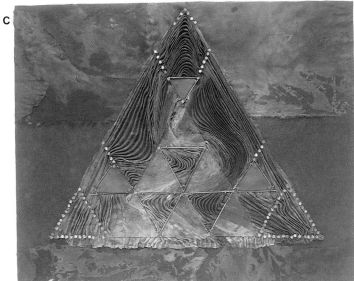

E

D

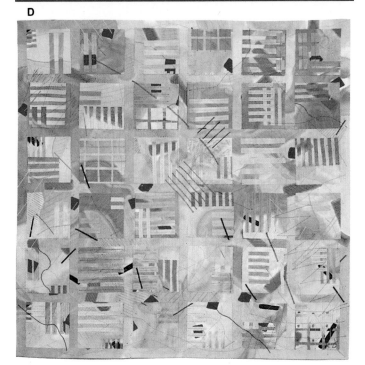

F

G

E

Angelika Sempel-Kleinlosen
First School Day
Direct application on silk; 20 by
23 cm.

F

Marna Goldstein Brauner
Tophole
Photo silk screen, stenciling,
stamping, painting; linen, beads,
sequins; 48 by 38 inches.
Photo: E.G. Schempf.
*I juxtapose symbolic imagery to
create a personal narrative. I
am inspired by Coptic and
Jewish ceremonial textiles.*

G

Dorothy Caldwell
Landstat
Wax resist, discharge, applique;
cotton, applied gold leaf,
acrylic; 50 by 18 feet. Photo:
Nelson Vigneult.
*This piece was made for the
lobby of the Red Deer Arts
Centre in Alberta. Quilted by
three quilting groups, it is
based on land forms in Alberta
as seen from the air.*

A
Suzel Back
Si Dolce Il Tormento
Batik on cotton; 52 by 65
inches. Photo: Daniel Roussel.

B

Carter Smith
Fuchsias
Discharge dye on silk chiffon;
44 by 84 inches.

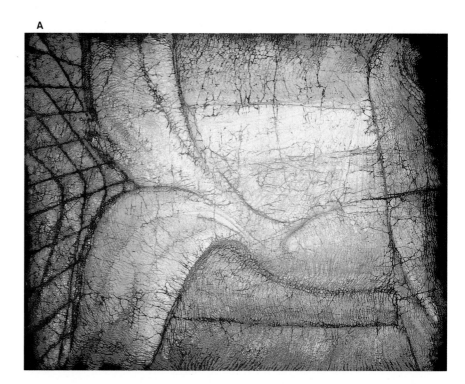

A

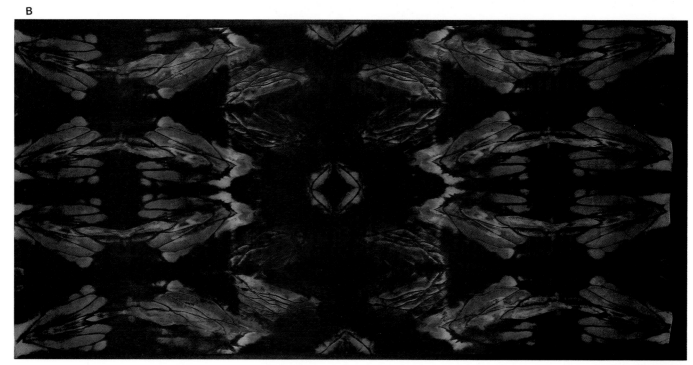

B

NEEDLEWORK

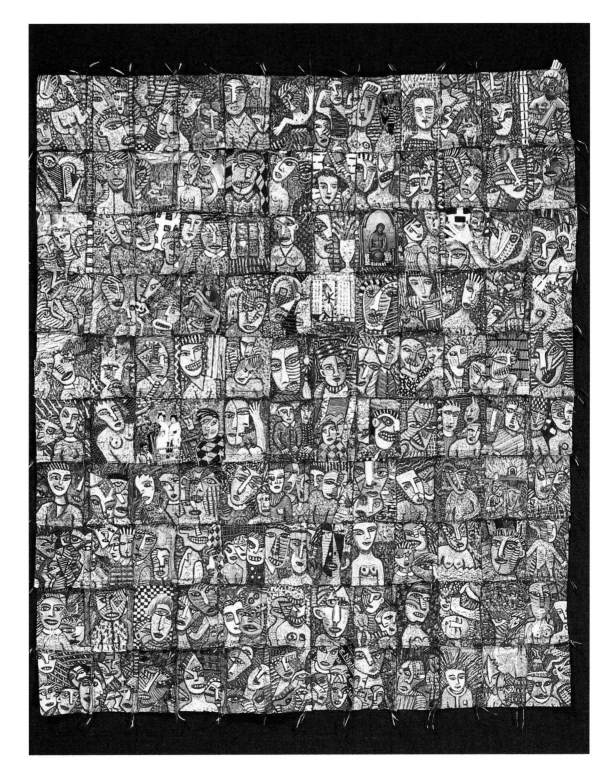

Mary Bero
Mind Spasms III
Painted, stitched; paper,
acrylics, fabric, thread; 11 by
12½ inches. Photo: Jim
Wildeman / Skylight Studios.

A

Connie Lehman
*Artists With Beasts,
Sleeping-Sleeping*

Igolochkoy (Russian needle
punch); cotton, silk, metallic
thread on silk; 5¼ by 3¾ by 1
inches.

B

Lynn Stearns
Sanctuary

Knotless netting; Persian wool,
assorted fabrics; 6 inches in
diameter, 6 inches high. Photo:
Roger Stearns.

*One image and inspiration that
has been carried over from my
painting is the tree and the line
movement it suggests.*

A

B

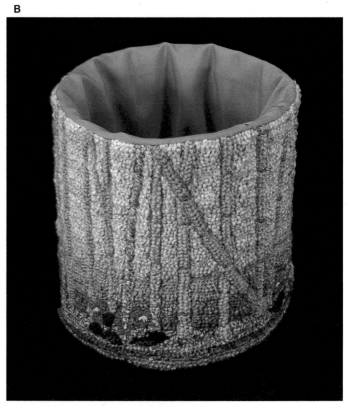

C

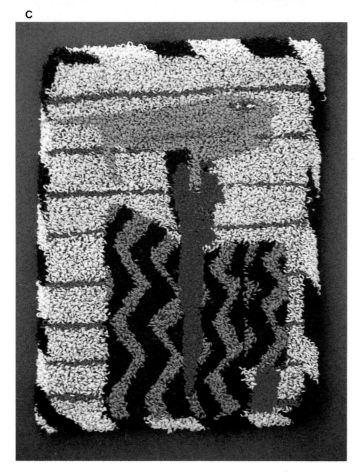

D

156

E

F

G

C

Connie Lehman

Woody Heads for Paradise

Igolochkoy (Russian needle punch); cotton, silk thread on silk noil; 3¾ by 5 by 1 inches.

D

Arlyn Ende

Pots & Kettles Beach, Block Island

Tapeta, hooked variations; wool, mohair, rayon yarns, fabric; 71 by 73 inches. Photo: Gary Dryden.

A soft, changeable, suggestive, vibrant, touchable salmagundi of yarns and fabrics companionably combined by hooking, tufting, punch needling and other variations on a threaded theme to enliven a favorite reverie: my summers on an enchanted island off the coast of New England.

E

Carrie Jacobson

Los Alamos

Tufted tapestry; wool; 52 by 38 inches.

F

Patti Handley

Floating Landscape

Sheared and sculpted punch hooking; wool yarns; 84 by 45 by 1 inches.

The changing color and patterns of the fertile San Joaquin Valley offer unending inspiration. This work lifts the plowed fields up and out into a floating mist of light and shadow.

G

Martha Donovan Opdahl

Jigsaw Puzzle

Tufting, ikat; wool; 79 by 48 inches.

My work is an effort to present felt tensions as visual tensions. I try to show what life feels like, yet create a work with a life of its own.

A

A

Salley Mavor
Feeding Chickens

Embroidery, stenciled fabric, wrapping; fabric, cardboard, wool yarn, fiberfill, embroidery floss, artificial leaves and flowers, wire, wood; 22 by 24 by 1 inches.

B

Patti Handley
Bright Valley

Sheared and sculpted punch hooking; wool yarns; 99 by 55 by 1¼ inches. Photo: E.Z. Smith.

C

Rosita Johanson
The Beach

Machine applique; cotton, cotton blends; 8 by 6½ inches. Photo: Lenscape Incorporated.

My work is my love and life. The design and inspiration are my dreams. The function is to enjoy.

D

Rosita Johanson
Coming Home

Machine applique; cotton, cotton blends; 8 by 6 inches. Photo: Lenscape Incorporated.

E

Martha Cole
Railroad Crossing

Applique, free-hand machine embroidery; assorted fabrics, fabric paints, cotton threads; 72 by 36 by 1½ inches. Photo: C. Pittenger.

This landscape is based on southern Saskatchewan country.

B

C

D

F

E

F
Salley Mavor
Fall
Embroidery, wrapping, dyeing; fabric, buttons, wire, wood, beads, ribbon, embroidery floss, socks, cardboard; 28 by 20 by 1 inches.

G
Roslyn Logsdon
Summer Porch
Rug hooking; woolen strips; 44 by 34½ inches. Photo: Linda Zandler.

G

A

B

C

D

E

F

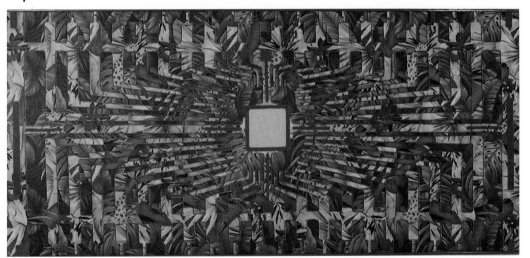

G

A

F. Jane Cameron

Indian Princess

Stitchery; wool, acrylic; 23¾ by 38 inches. Photo: Indefinite Arts.

B

Cindy Hickok

The Farmer Takes a Wife

Machine embroidery on soluble fabric, which is then dissolved; cotton sewing thread; 5 by 5 inches.

C

Charlotte Kennedy

Bugaku

Applique, hand and machine embroidery, quilting; linen/cotton prints, moire, felt, silk threads, beads; 20 by 24 by 1 inches. Photo: Bill R. Jans.

The title of this piece refers to the ancient court dances performed in kabuki theater.

D

Gigi Benanti

Self Portrait

Stitched, woven, painted; fabric, pencil, beads, threads; 15 by 15 inches, framed.

My needleworks are drawn from past realistic experiences which are now pure and emotionally colored. They reflect the deepest emotions of my inner dyslexic personality.

E

Diane Fitzgerald

Ardebeil

Needlepoint; wool, mono canvas; 39 by 19 inches.

F

Martha Cole

Silicon Connection

Applique; cotton fabrics; 96 by 48 by 1½ inches. Photo: I. Berg Muller.

G

Jo Consoli

Ragsie's Rug

Dyed felt applique, quilted with yarn; 39 by 23 inches.

Rags is the cat who doesn't get to curl up on his rug.

A

Andrea Deimel
Sitting Looking

Satin stitch embroidery; muslin, cotton embroidery floss.

I love creating these pieces and am always coming up with ideas garnered from numerous sources.

B

Gloria E. Crouse
Creme-de-la-Creme

Rug hooking variations, sculptured, cut and uncut loops; wool/metal elements on linen ground; 79 by 56 by 1½ inches. Photo: Chris Eden.

The first in a continuing series of 2-part art rugs. The sections adjust to many diverse shapes and sizes: together, apart, side by side, back to back, etc.

C

Mary G. Fry
Triptych

Pearl cotton counted stitches on linen ground; 24 by 24 inches, each.

D

Moyra McNeill
Reflections I

Free machine cutwork, spraying, applique; cotton poplin bonded onto stiff Vilene; lurex; 27 by 33 inches.

E

Louise Jamet
Variations sur le Carre

Embroidery; cotton, thread; 14 by 14 inches. Photo: Jacques Lavallee.

F

Janet Leszczynski
Transmutation

Stitchery; cotton thread on silk; 12 by 12 inches.

I believe the spirit of this work acknowledges and achieves a kinship with music.

G

Astri Raestad Synnes
Disarmed or Humiliated Knife

Machine embroidery on water-dissolvable material; silk, sewing thread, watercolor; 13 by 36 cm.

Old weapons, shields, knives, and swords have been my main source of inspiration for the last year. I have, in my works, disarmed them even more than they already are, but I have given them color and tried to keep their dignity.

B

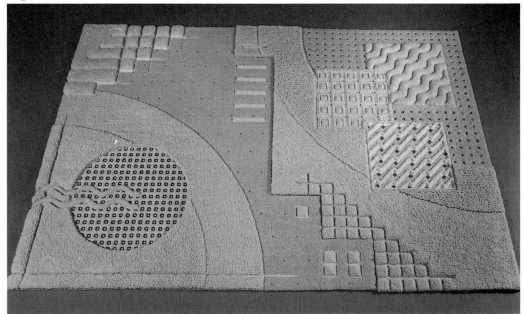

C

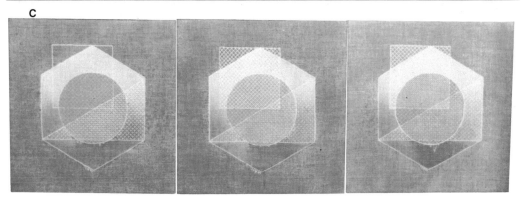

D

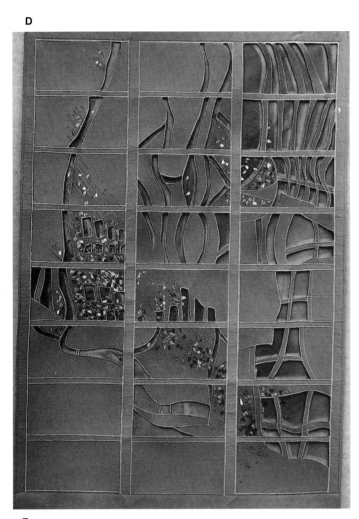

E

F

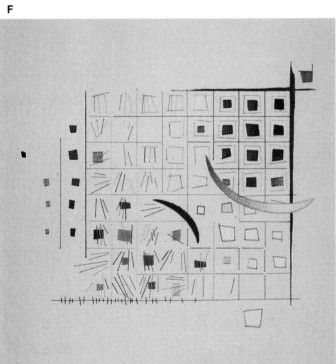

G

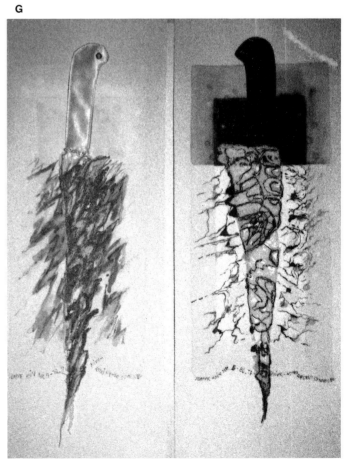

A

B

C

D

A

Jan Ross-Manley
Frangipanny
Machine embroidery, applique, hand stitching; cotton, wool, satin rouleau, decals; 51 by 61 cm.
An idyll about a favorite pet and country living.

B

Mary Bero
Zebra Lady
Embroidery; cotton, cotton floss; 3¾ by 4 inches. Photo: Jim Wildeman/Skylight Studios.

E

F

G

C
Caroline Dahl
Hiya-Hawaya
Embroidery; cotton floss; 12 by 14 by 1 inches. Photo: Stone Photo.

D
Caroline Dahl
Kentucky Sampler
Embroidery; cotton floss; 12 by 14 by 1 inches. Photo: Stone Photo.

E
Renie Breskin Adams
Teatime
Stitchery, knotting, crochet; cotton threads on cotton canvas; 9⅜ by 10⅜ by ¾ inches.

I like to construct surfaces that are alive with variations of color and fabric structure. My ultimate purpose is narrative—I make art in order to tell my stories, both real and imaginary.

F
Renie Breskin Adams
David
Stitchery, knotting, crochet; cotton threads on cotton canvas; 12 by 13½ by ⅝ inches.

G
Maribeth Baloga
A Place Untouched By David Attenborough
Embroidery; cotton and silk on muslin; 4½ by 4 inches.

A

Elly Smith

Cross Stitch Conflict

Counted thread embroidery;
hardanger, cotton thread; 42 by
30 inches. Photo: Steve Meltzer.

*This is an attempt to integrate
my various identities: mother,
wife, artist, tennis player,
fantasy person. I also wanted
the design to announce, "Look,
I am an embroidery, a thread
and fabric phenomenon!"
Therefore, note the color code
numbers.*

B

Margaret Cusack

Country Celebration

Machine applique, fabric
collage; cotton, silk, corduroy,
satin; 29 by 22 inches. Photo:
Ron Breland.

C

Susanne Klinke

Lace-rate

Lace, machine embroidery;
cotton; 120 by 250 cm.

D

Elisabeth Weissensteiner

*Andachtsbild (Devotion
Picture)*

Handwoven linen, embroidered
with linen thread and nickel
gold thread; 49 by 58 cm.

*One of my goals is to
investigate the matriarchal
implications in religion. Fiber, a
material with a long female
history, is the perfect medium
for me to express the
necessary intensity.*

A

B

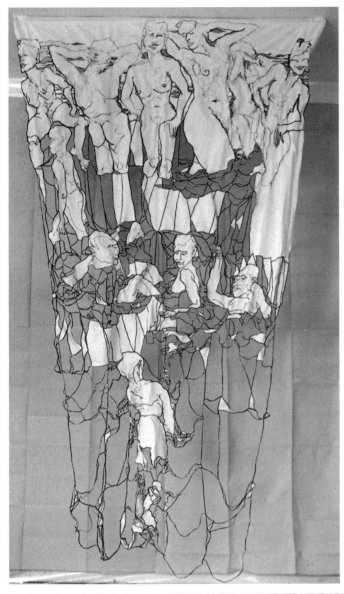

D

C

A

Linda Lochmiller

My Life

Reverse and 3-dimensional applique; cotton; 35 by 25 inches. Photo: Roger Vandiver.

This piece is about integrating my work and my child into one life.

B

Star Moxley

No! Not the Dark Dress!

Applique; cotton, cotton/poly chintz; 70 by 48 inches. Photo: Michael Cordell.

C

Joyce Heinicke

Halcyon

Embroidery; silk and wool threads on silk; 13⅛ by 12⅛ inches. Photo: Chromatech Corp.

D

Maribeth Baloga

Alone in Exotic Places

Embroidery, fabric painting; cotton and silk on linen; 12 by 14 inches.

E

Sally Broadwell

Pink Salmon

Pieced, quilted, beaded; fabrics, yarn, ribbon, beads, other embellishments; 11 by 11 inches.

A

B

C

D

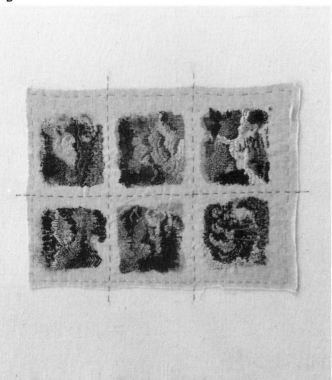

E

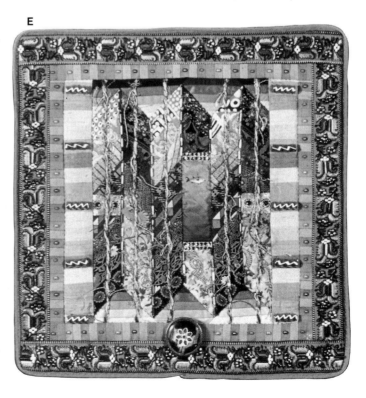

A

Richard Box

Poppies and Daisies

Collage, machine and hand
embroidery; assorted fabrics
and threads; 10 by 6 inches.

B

Mary Snyder Behrens

Rainbow Sleeves

Machine stitching, applique,
collage; fabric, thread,
ribbons; 30 by 20 inches.

A

B

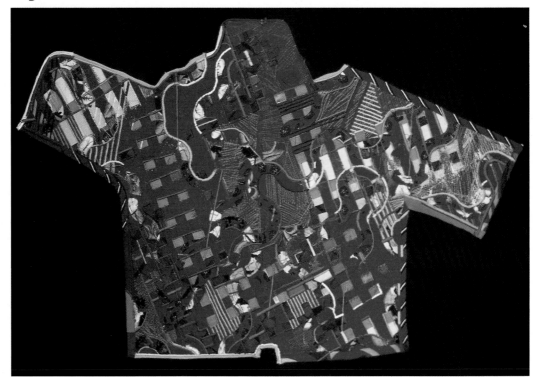

DIVERSIONS

Susan Shie
Elvira on the Nile
Painting, stitching, stuffing, quilting, pocket-making; canvas, fabric, acrylic paint, yarn, floss, found objects; 9 by 8½ feet.

My work is a pictorial diary of my life, but I use made-up symbolism often. Elvira is the big dog in this piece—our black lab. The pink car is made of the dress I wore for graduate school graduation last year.

A

Lynn DiNino

Finger Lickin' Good

Fabric over welded steel, rubber, plastic ants; 40 by 24 by 42 inches.

Why animals? Because they're beautiful, can be so easily personified, are silly at times, have curves, and come in such a variety of packages., In these animals I try to instill fun, and if YOU smile, I'm really pleased and feel I've done my job.

B

Julia Blackwood

General Reception

Free-hand machine quilting, machine and hand applique; dyed fabrics, leather, metallic threads, silk lame, telephone receiver and cords, paper clips, stamps, keys, etc.; 26 by 31½ by 6 inches.

A

B

C

Margot Strand Jensen
Topsy-Turvy Doll: John & Yoko

Xerox transfer on satin, machine pieced, stuffed, hand beaded, attached found objects; 21½ inches long.

This is the second doll in a series I created in tribute to John Lennon. It is a doll all about love between two people, about beauty, tragedy, and memories.

D

Lois Schklar
Figure with Birch Face

Stitching, dyeing; upholstery material, Chinese soup sticks, silk, birch; 3½ by 24 by 1½ inches. Photo: Bruce Hogg.

The themes I address in my work concern the female as the embodiment of magical/spiritual powers and intellectual/emotional struggles.

E

Lois Schklar
Figure with Birch

Sewing, painting; cotton, silk, dyes, birch bark; 3½ by 23 by 1½ inches. Photo: Bruce Hogg.

F

Ingrid Dijkers
Titania

Hand and machine sewn, torn fabrics; acetate taffeta, cotton, nylon; 14 by 35 by 13 inches.

D

E

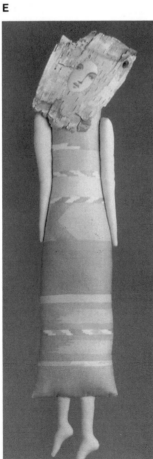

A

B

C

D

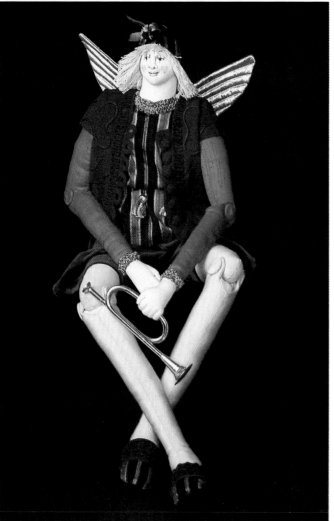

A

Nikki Chabot

Azzeltine

Soft sculpture, embroidery; assorted fabrics, buttons, bells, beads; 4 by 8 by 3 inches.

Photo: Bill Brennan.

For me, humor is a big part of doll-making. My dolls are adult characters, their personalities equal measures of reality, fantasy, and humor.

B

Sine McCann

Des Struction & Vicky Tim

Hand construction, machine stitching; cottons, wools, synthetics, ribbons, threads, plastic; 110 cm. tall.

Des Struction represents the destruction mankind has happily committed on Earth, e.g. extinction of animals, use of nuclear weapons. Vicky was the essence of life, but is now a corpse, another victim of Des's.

C

Akira Blount

Angel With Horn

Soft sculpture; cotton knit, silk, velveteen, vintage jersey, gold synthetic; 6 by 24 by 6 inches. Photo: Laughlin Photography.

D

Akira Blount

Peasant Woman

Soft sculpture; cottons, linen, antique lace, handwoven cotton, cotton knit; 8 by 29 by 8 inches. Photo: Laughlin Photography.

E

Linda Liu Behar

At Loose Ends

Machine pieced and quilted, embellished; cottons, cotton blends, rayon; 121 by 42 by 1½ inches. Photo: David Caras.

A fantasy kite, this piece has plenty of "loose ends" to flutter in the breeze.

F

Brent Brown

Prairie Window

Willow, tamarisk, royal palm, screen; 22 by 36 by 16 inches. Photo: Julie Bubar.

G

Lotte Kent

Italian Market

Frame loom weaving; wool, linen; 7 by 4½ inches.

I like to depict colorful scenes of my daily life with a little whimsy thrown in.

E

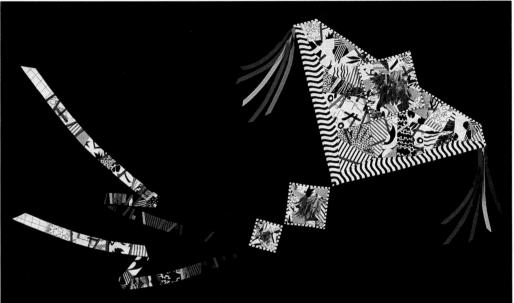

F

G

A

A
Eda E. Bannister
John

Tapestry; cotton; 5½ by 3¾ inches.

My works are based on my photography and portraiture.

B
Lydia Predominate
Maquette for Solid Speech Puzzle—Keyword: Tessitura

Emulsified canvas, silk, acrylic, threads, cotton string, felt layers; 185 by 110 by 25 cm.

C
Sue Watson
Tapa Gold

Paper stencil, silk screen; open weave canvas, wood, aluminum; 6 feet in diameter.

D
Andrea V. Uravitch
Bird Dog

Crochet and sewn covering over welded and constructed base; goat hair, wool, cotton fiber, steel; 36 by 29 by 9½ inches.

B

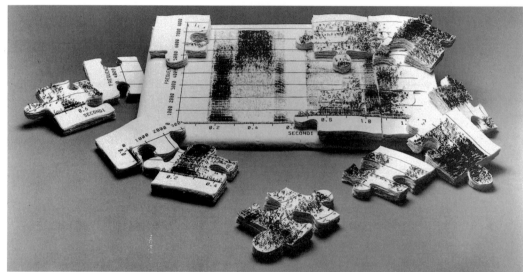

C

D

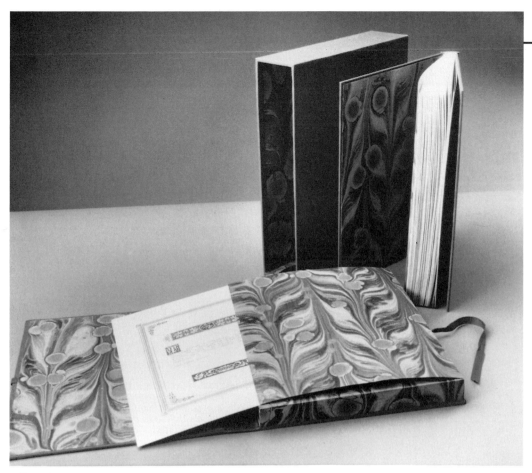

Linda Nelson Johnson
A Study in Victorian Presentation
Marbleizing, embossing, watercolor, handmade construction; 12 by 9¼ by 2½ inches. Photo: Lourdes Sodari-Smith.

F

Ruth Banta
Vanity Fantasy
Crochet, sewing; mixed yarns, fabric, mylar, found objects; 36 by 55 by 24 inches.

F

A

John L. Skau

Fido

Locker hooking, applique; rug canvas, assorted fabrics, string, foam rubber; 71 by 59 by 1 inches.

This carpet depicts my neighbor's dog. It is the first in a series dealing with "life in the big city."

B

Joni Bamford

Barn Cottage

Weaving, crochet, applique, stitchery; 12 by 24 by 6 inches.

This is a 3-D portrait of my home and workspace.

C

John L. Skau

Floor Runner

Locker hooking, applique, couching; rug canvas, assorted fabrics, string, vinyl, seagrass, paint, plasti-dip; 42 by 50 by 2 inches.

This carpet is a self-portrait.

A

B

C

Barbara Klaer and Judith Klaer
Electric Cat
Hand painting on silk noil.
Photo: George C. Anderson.

We work as a team—Judy sews and I dye. Before I begin, Judy has already cut the shape and put in some seams, so I have a shaped canvas. This enables me to design with both the garment shape and the body to wear it clearly in mind.

A

Ann Williamson Hyman
Grey and Green Suit
Applique, piecing; silk,
Guatemalan cotton ikat. Photo:
Anthony Rush Ledbetter.

B

Ann Williamson Hyman
Purple and Black Grid Coat
Piecing, applique; wool. Photo:
Anthony Rush Ledbetter.

C

Patricia Wilmott Novarr
Woman's reversible coat
16-shaft straight twill; wool.
Photo: Luca Aponte.

D

Ann Williamson Hyman
Grey jacket with charged applique
Piecing, applique; wool, silk.
Photo: Anthony Rush Ledbetter.

A

B

D

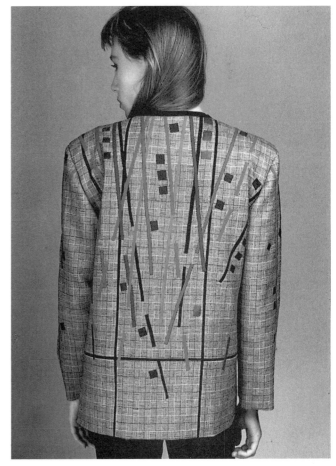

A

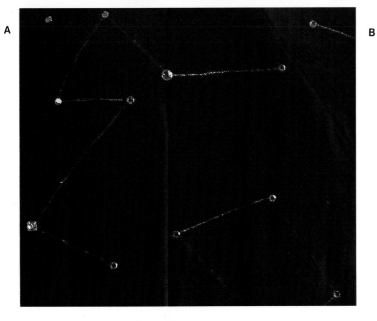

B

C

D

A

Gayle E. Edgerton
Constellation Coat
Embroidery, beading, sewing; velvet, satin stripe silk chiffon, silver thread, rhinestones. Photo: A.D. Wessling.

B

Julie Silletti
Red strip pieced coat with checkerboard and turquoise accents. Photo: Jon Bolton.

C

Bonnie Benson
Jewels of India
Machine piecing, hand applique and quilting; cotton, silk.

D

Elizabeth Garver
Stormy Weather #1
Hand painting, piecing, machine applique; silk noil, silk pongee. Photo: Richard Gray.

E

Jeanne Brenholts
Salad Dressing
Color Xerox transfer, machine piecing, applique; satin, color Xerox copies of lettuce, radishes, rhubarb, lemon, strawberries.

E

F

A

B

C

D

A
Ursula Mennerich
Ariane evening gown
Hand painting on silk satin.
Photo: Martin Veth, Munich.

B
Sandra Galloway
London Fog Gone Crazy
Hand painting, silk screen, lamination, construction; silk, vinyl. Photo: Eric Beldowski.

C
Mary Risseeuw
Black and White Cape
Hand drawing with dental syringe; cotton. Photo: George Tarbay.

D
Joce Yanni
Deco Feelings
Hand painting on silk crepe de chine. Photo: Robert Lakstigala.

E
Barbara Klaer and Judith Klaer
Cattails
Hand painting on silk noil.
Photo: George C. Anderson.

F
Elizabeth Garver
Landscape Series Jacket
Hand painting, piecing, machine applique; silk noil, silk pongee. Photo: Richard Gray.

G
Jeanne Brenholts
Fan-Fare
Color Xerox transfer, machine piecing and applique; satin, fans, lace doilies.

E

F
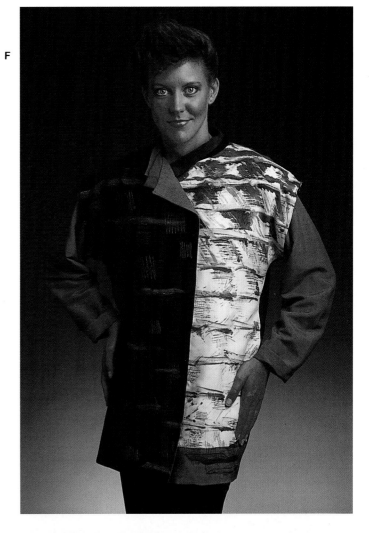

G

A

Sandra Galloway
Repetitious Meeting
Silk screened and hand painted silk georgette. Photo: Merina Donath.

B

Louise Landry
Dance Dress
Direct painting with bamboo brushes on silk charmeuse. Photo: Kim Gendron.

C

Marion Helbing-Muecke
Cologne Cathedral
Mixed media, resist dyeing; silk crepe de chine. Photo: P. Clemens.

As a designer and artist, I always feel, above all, the joy of creation.

D

Gayle E. Edgerton
Wolf Print Ensemble
Silk screen, sewing; rayon challis, cotton twill. Photo: A.D. Wessling.

E

Judith Stein
A Trip Down the Nile
Dye painting with rubber stamps on cotton. Photo: Joe Watson.

B

C

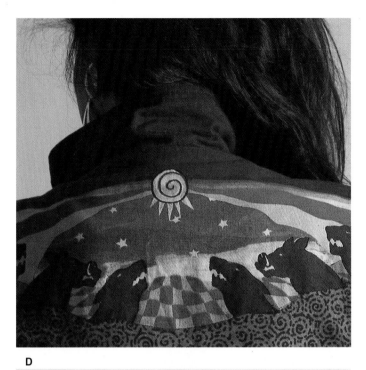

D

E

A

Ann Welch

Rose For A Dark Lady

Batik, full immersion dyeing; silk taffeta. Photo: Schecter Lee.

This is a full skirt with a complex design which intertwines Elizabethan quotes, tea roses, hearts, and lace-like patterns in close detail.

B

Joce Yanni

Waves and Checkerboards

Hand painting on silk. Photo: Robert Lakstigala.

C

Sandi Wright

Mi Corazon dress

Handwoven and hand painted silk. Photo: Pat Berrett.

This dress was inspired by the New Mexico symbols of the Spanish cross and "mi corazon."

D

Mary G. Fry

Blouse

Counted and free form stitches; linen, silver leaf.

E

Brenda Rolls

Sleeveless Jacket

Dyed and felted fleece, suede leather.

F

Animalistic Outerwear

Felt Coat

Dyed and felted wool. Photo: Rick Convery.

A

B

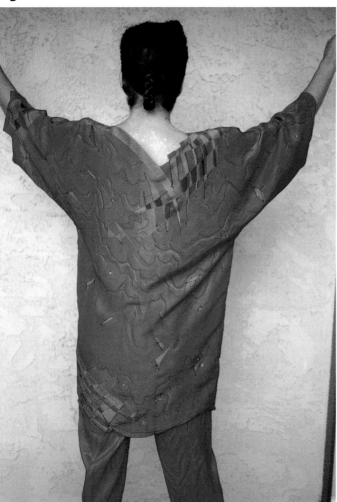

C

D

E

F

A

B

C

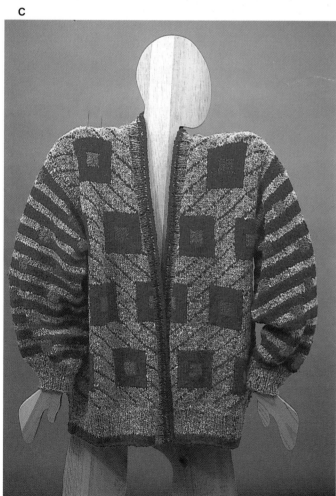

D

A
Sheila Sharp
Poncho/Coat
Machine knitting and crochet; wool. Photo: M. Siebert.
This is my first attempt at breaking away from traditional coat shapes.

B
Marion Helbing-Muecke
Endless Mud Flats
Machine knitted in one piece; alpaca, silk. Photo: P. Clemens.

C
Linda Dobris
Jacket with Squares
Hand knitted wool, cotton chenille, mohair. Photo: Susan Schiller.

D
Arta-Cloaks
Untitled tunic dress
Handloomed, hand dyed, hand painted rayon, viscose, and cotton. Photo: Claude Lazzara.
Our garments are completed entirely in combinations of white yarns. The finished garments are then hand dyed and painted.

E
Patricia Wheeler
Cat Sweater
Machine knit wool.
This sweater was designed and worn as a Halloween costume. My cat was my model and inspiration.

F
Ellen Liss
Lightning Flight
Machine knitting, crochet, applique; pearl cotton.
This piece depicts a "war of the worlds" between land creatures and sky creatures.

E

F

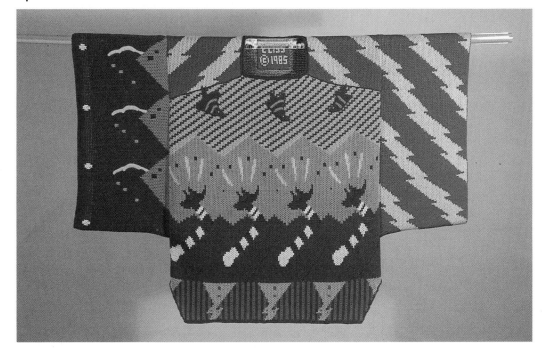

A

B

C

D

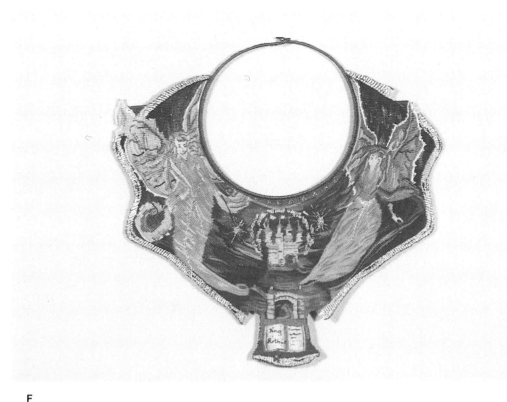

Tapestry woven; hand dyed wool, cotton. Photo: Untitled Fine Arts.

I am highly influenced by the peoples of indigenous America, the ways they express their enjoyment of colors, patterns, and textures, and their application of these in their everyday lives.

D
Renata Brink
Shawl

Ikat dyeing, 8-shaft twill; silk.

E
Elmyra Tidwell
One Brief Shining Moment, Camelot

Tapestry woven; cotton, silk, gold and silver bullion thread. Photo: Brad Fricke.

It took 400 hours to complete this piece.

F
Theodora Elston
Artist at Work

Painting, dyeing, embroidery, paper bead making, macrame; silk and cotton embroidery thread, silk fabric, textile paints, dyed waxed nylon, button.

This was a fun piece to make out of the clutter that inevitably accumulates on the top of my desk. Instead of fighting the mess, I used it!

G
Janet Long
Untitled

Knotted nylon carpet thread. Photo: John Long.

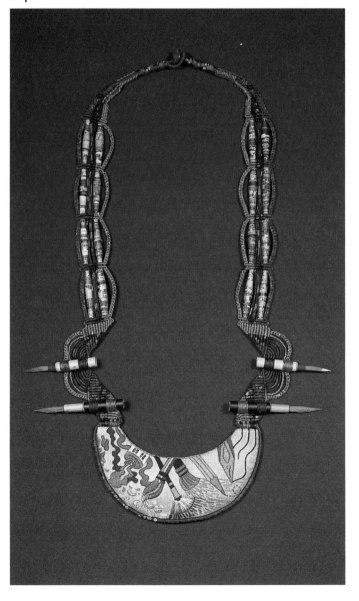

A
Denise Hanlon
Meadow Dance

Woven, complementary warp face patterning, five-loop squared braid, Vandyke stitch join, twined balls; hand dyed wool.

B
Ira Ono
Single Earring

Mixed media; treated paper. Photo: Sherry Siegal.

C
Doris Louie
Bag and legal case

A

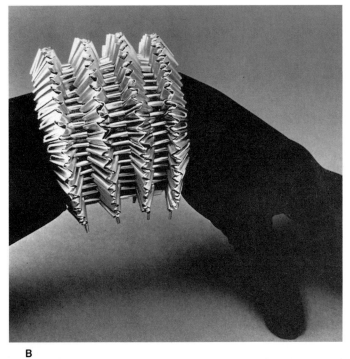

B

C

D

E

A
Grace Hamilton
Neckpiece I
Intertwined needle-woven
sections; cotton, nickel-plated
closures.

B
Gina Westergard
Untitled
Continuous wire weave;
sterling silver, patinated copper
tubing.

C
Keiko Kobayashi
The Neck Piece No. 2
Peruvian scaffolding; linen.
*I invented the puzzle weave
using the Peruvian scaffolding
technique. First I weave the
ring on the frame
independently; then I weave the
next ring, inserting the former
ring just before finishing.*

D
Louisa Simons
Hippari Jacket
Shibori, wrapping, braiding;
cotton, cotton padding.

E
Dr. Nancy Zimmerman Kotch
Old Rose Patterned Kimono
Overshot weave; wool; 55 by 55
inches, mounted.

A

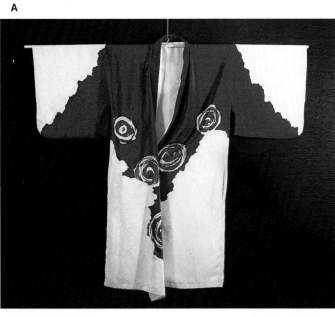 

B

C

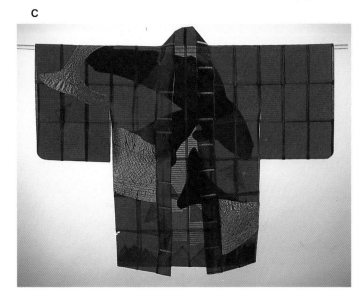 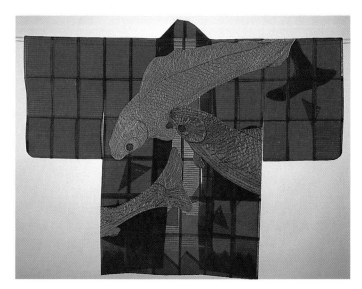

196

D

E

C

Janny Burghardt-Pezaro
Fische Kimono
Hand and machine piecing; machine embroidery, hand applique; microfiche, silver lame, thread. Photo: Jay Bachemin.

D

Leonore Alaniz
Alamo
Tabby weave; rayon, wool. Photo: Walter Jebbe.

E

Barbara Simon and Marjorie Hoeltzel
Keso Coat
Plain weave, inlay, stitchery, strip piecing; hand dyed wool and silk, wool fabric.
This coat was inspired by the Keso forest in Japan. We attempted to capture the many shades of green and delicate touches of cinnabar.

F

Leonore Alaniz
Happy Sweater from the collection, "Homage to George Seurat"
Eight-harness Bronson weave; wool.

A

Louise Desaulniers
Old Dream
Hand painting; silk pongee and silk crepe de chine.

B

Louise Desaulniers
Our Own Jail
Hand painting; silk pongee and silk crepe de chine.

F

197

A

Barbara Simon
Silk Road Fantasy
Broken twill and tapestry weaves; silks. Photo: Kurt Eckhard.

This coat has a light, free feeling that represents a Silk Road fantasy journey.

B

Barbara Hiles
Chemise
Rosepath variation weave; rayon, silk, cotton. Photo: Cosimo Zaccaria.

My interest has been the interrelationship of color with texture . . . With the aid of a streamlined production handloom and computer-assisted designs, I have been able to expedite the process of creating new cloth.

C

Diana Sanderson
Ikat ensemble
Ikat on silk; fashion accessories by Paula O'Keefe. Photo: Margaret Inkster.

D

Deborah Cross
Woman's jacket
Inlay weave; cotton, silk, rayon. Photo: Mehosh.

A

B

C

D

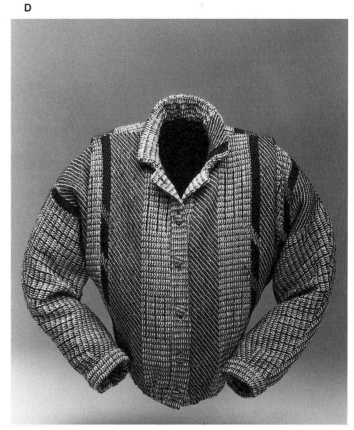

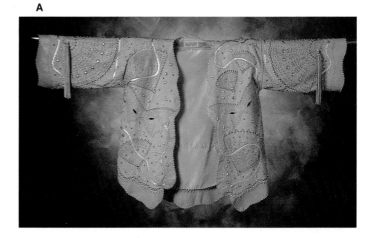

A

A

Jan Faulkner-Wagoner
Masks and Fans

Applique, beading, punching; embossed calf, metallic leather, beads.

Both masks and fans are romantic symbols, hiding mysteries to be discovered.

B

Jan Faulkner-Wagoner
OZ: An Australian Walkabout

Applique, reverse applique, beading, studding; metallic, kangaroo, and calf leathers, beads, shells.

This is a journal piece, recording my experience from eight months in Australia.

C

Robert Hillestad
Celebration Coat XII

Knitted with shag technique, dyed and painted; rayon, assorted fibers.

D

Susan Osmond
Risen

Airbrushed dyes on silk pongee. Photo: Gerry Fenclau.

This work was created for the feast of Easter; colors and techniques were used to create a sense of movement and light.

E

Marjorie Hoeltzel
Raindrops Keep Falling on My Head

Clear plastic, vinyl, nylon, mylar, metallic stars. Photo: Red Elf.

B

C

D

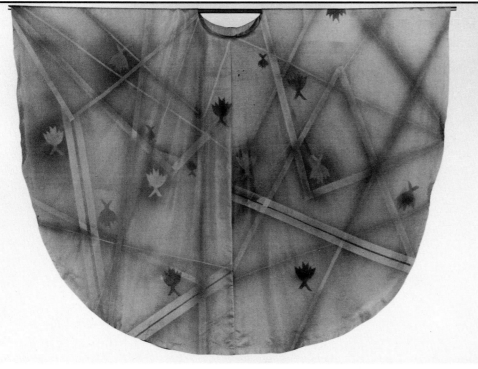

E

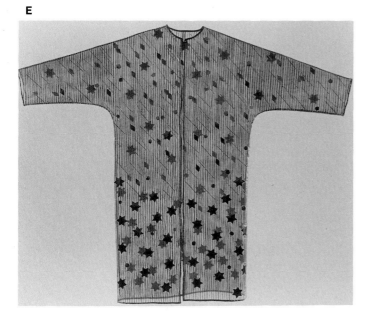

F

INDEX

A

Ann M. Adams   112
Edmonds, Washington

Renie Breskin Adams   165
DeKalb, Illinois

Leonore Alaniz   197
San Francisco, California

Donna Albert   119
Lancaster, Pennsylvania

Barbara J. Allen   92
Sandy Hook, Connecticut

Faye Anderson   133, 138
Denver, Colorado

Animalistic Outerwear   189
Edgartown, Massachusetts

Janice Anthony   147
Brooks, Maine

Arta-Cloaks   190
Buffalo, New York

Ellen Athens   27
Mendocino, California

Susan Atwell   151
Valparaiso, Indiana

Ilze Aviks   29
Durango, Colorado

B

Suzel Back   154
Montreal, Quebec, Canada

Michael Bailot   104
Taos, New Mexico

Maribeth Baloga   165, 169
Van Nuys, California

Joni Bamford   178
Rutland, Leicester, England

Eda E. Bannister   176
Saskatoon, Saskatchewan,
Canada

Ruth Banta   177
Cincinnati, Ohio

Cynthia Barbone   52
Greenwich, New York

Elizabeth A. Bard   63
Orono, Maine

Dorothy Gill Barnes   102, 107
Worthington, Ohio

Roxana Bartlett   142
Boulder, Colorado

Lynn Basa   29
Seattle, Washington

Barbara Bate   72
Miramonte, California

Marilyn Beal   151
Worcester, Massachusetts

Judy Becker   117
Newton, Massachusetts

Pamela E. Becker   70
Marcellus, New York

Linda Liu Behar   175
Lexington, Massachusetts

Mary Snyder Behrens   170
Cincinnati, Ohio

Nancy Belfer   33
Buffalo, New York

Gigi Benanti   160
Norwalk, Connecticut

Bonnie Benson   182
Chicago, Illinois

Christine Benson   9, 22
Ann Arbor, Michigan

Patty Bentley   123
Newberg, Oregon

Yael Bentovim   88, 89
Los Angeles, California

Julier Berner   130
Eugene, Oregon

Mary Bero   155, 164
Madison, Wisconsin

Julia Blackwood   172
Easton, Maryland

Akira Blount   174
Bybee, Tennessee

Danielle Bodine   106
Birmingham, Michigan

Ilse Bolle   79
Palatine, Illinois

Bonni Boren   40
San Francisco, California

Richard Box   170
London, England

Odette Brabec   30
Highland Park, Illinois

Jennifer Bradley   144
Lugarno, New South Wales
Australia

Pat Bramhall   109
Croghan, New York

Ann Brauer   128
Charlemont, Massachusetts

Marna Goldstein Brauner   153
Edmonton, Alberta,
Canada

Donna Caryn Braverman   71
Scottsdale, Arizona

Jeanne Brenholts   183, 185
Pittsburgh, Pennsylvania

Renata Brink   192
Hamburg, West Germany

Sally Broadwell   169
St. Augustine, Florida

Liese Bronfenbrenner   143
Ithaca, New York

Tim Brooks   147
Baddeck, Nova Scotia
Canada

Brent Brown   175
Crest, California

Victoria Brown   84
London, England

Laura Militzer Bryant   150
Orchard Park, New York

Diane Burchard   72
Santa Fe, New Mexico

Janny Burghardt-Pezaro   196
Cincinnati, Ohio

Deborah L. Burton   92
Brooks, Kentucky

Ruth Bilowus Butler   36
Goleta, California

C

Dorothy Caldwell   153
Hastings, Ontario
Canada

Kay Campbell   45
Ashland, Oregon

F. Jane Cameron   160
Calgary, Alberta
Canada

Joyce Marquess Carey   113, 128
Madison, Wisconsin

Erika G. Carter   129
Bellevue, Washington

Nikki Chabot   174
Edmonton, Alberta
Canada

Marilyn McKenzie Chaffee   124
San Diego, California

Karen Chapnick   42
Vancouver, British Columbia,
Canada

Vikki Berman Chenette   134
Jersey City, New Jersey

Colleen Christie-Putnam   89
Oakland, California

Susanne Clawson   94
Tallahassee, Florida

Barbara Clemens   62
Koln, West Germany

Morgan Clifford   59
Stillwater, Minnesota

Susie Cobbledick   61
Kent, Ohio

Martha Cole   159, 161
Lumsden, Saskatchewan,
Canada

Mary Rawcliffe Colton   151
Albuquerque, New Mexico

Jo Consoli   161
Pittsburgh, Pennsylvania

Jenny Kathleen Cook   23
Truro, Cornwall, England

Janet Crafer   21
Dorrington, Lincoln, England

Barbara L. Crane   121
Lexington, Massachusetts

Deborah Cross   199
Ithaca, New York

Gloria E. Crouse   162
Olympia, Washington

Margaret Cusack   166
Brooklyn, New York

D

Caroline Dahl   164
Lexington, Kentucky

Carolyn A. Dahl   144
Houston, Texas

Dave Davis   98, 110
Crest, California

Michael Davis   101
Jacksonville, Florida

Andrea Deimel 162
Worcester, Massachusetts

Louise Desaulniers 196
Trois-Rivieres, Quebec,
Canada

Ingrid Dijkers 173
Plymouth, Michigan

Judith Dingle 66, 76
Toronto, Ontario, Canada

Lynn DiNino 172
Seattle, Washington

Linda Dobris 190
Davis, California

Allison Doherty 83
West Tisbury, Massachusetts

Ellen Roberts Dreibelbis 136
San Francisco, California

Donna Durbin 60
Houston, Texas

Monika Duthie 75, 145
Weston, Ontario, Canada

Lois Dvorak 96
Santa Fe, New Mexico

E

Henry Easterwood 40
Memphis, Tennessee

Jeanie Eberhardt 106, 108
Layton, New Jersey

Josee Ebner 63
Tuttwig, Switzerland

Carol Eckert 74
Tempe, Arizona

Barbara Eckhardt 65
New Bedford, Massachusetts

Joann Eckstut 78
New York, New York

Gayle E. Edgerton 182, 187
Ann Arbor, Michigan

Betty Edwards 61
Ithaca, New York

Sylvia H. Einstein 129
Belmont, Massachusetts

Monica Ellis 90
Atlanta, Georgia

Theodora Elston 36, 193
Oakland, California

Arlyn Ende 156
Bradyville, Tennessee

Nancy N. Erickson 117, 134
Missoula, Montana

Jamie Evrard 104
Vancouver, British Columbia,
Canada

F

Kathleen Moore Farling 100
Oxford, Ohio

Jan Faulkner-Wagoner 200
Harrisburg, Pennsylvania

Jane Fawkes 114, 117
West Vancouver,
British Columbia, Canada

Diane Fitzgerald 161
Minneapolis, Minnesota

Roberta Fountain 93
Chico, California

Hey Frey 88
Toronto, Ontario,
Canada

Mary G. Fry 162, 189
Summit, New Jersey

G

Sandra Galloway 184, 186
Toronto, Ontario
Canada

Elene Gamache 22, 23
Sillery, Quebec, Canada

Elizabeth Garver 183, 185
South Bend, Indiana

Rita Romanova Gekht 13
New York, New York

Ursula Gerber-Senger 130
Mannedorf, Switzerland

Murray Gibson 32
Calgary, Alberta, Canada

Sara Gilfert 90
Athens, Ohio

Katy Gilmore 121
Anchorage, Alaska

Suellen Glashausser 95
Highland Park, New Jersey

Nancy Goes 101
Denver, Colorado

Tricia Goldberg 10, 40
San Francisco, California

Lida Gordon 77
Louisville, Kentucky

Sue A. Goudy 52, 53
DeKalb, Illinois

Ruth Gowell 46
Falls Church, Virginia

Amy Grandt-Nielsen 84
Odense, Denmark

Linda Gray 117
N. Conway, New Hampshire

Laura Elizabeth Green 127
St. Petersburg, Florida

Louise Weaver Greene 21
Chevy Chase, Maryland

Lauren Gregersen-Brow 142
Ann Arbor, Michigan

Barbara Grenell 58
Burnsville, North Carolina

Elizabeth Griffin 68
Toronto, Ontario, Canada

Donna Guardino 84
Sonoma, California

Ida Irene Guldhammer 82
Copenhagen, Denmark

Marla Gunderson 64
Chicago, Illinois

Karen R. Gutowski 50
Putney, Vermont

H

Terri Hall 49, 59
Wagga Wagga, New So. Wales
Australia

Shirley Halverson 108
Gig Harbor, Washington

Grace Hamilton 194
Albuquerque, New Mexico

Michele R. Hamrick 34
Vacaville, California

Patti Handley 157, 158
Fresno, California

Denise Hanlon 192
Oakdale, California

Joan Harrell 59
Denton, Texas

Kaija Sanelma Harris 49
Saskatoon, Saskatchewan,
Canada

Marilyn Lawrance Harrison 149
Boca Raton, Florida

Molly Hart 43
Cloverdale, California

Joan Hausrath 151
E. Bridgewater, Massachusetts

Valerie Hearder 122
Mahone Bay, Nova Scotia,
Canada

Judy Wasserman Hearst 135
Milwaukee, Wisconsin

Joyce Heinicke 169
Wichita, Kansas

Marion Helbing-Muecke 186, 190
Wiesbaden, West Germany

Barbara Heller 12, 22, 25
Vancouver, British Columbia
Canada

Priscilla Henderson 102, 103
La Jolla, California

Scott Hendricksen 26
Memphis, Tennessee

Anneke Herrold 62
Greencastle, Indiana

Jean Hewes 140
Fort Worth, Texas

Deborah Hickman 20
Mahone, Nova Scotia,
Canada

Cindy Hickok 160
Sugarland, Texas

Deborah Hildreth 16
New York, New York

Barbara Hiles 198
Pittsburgh, Pennsylvania

Robert Hillestad 200
Lincoln, Nebraska

Marjorie Hoeltzel 197, 201
St. Louis, Missouri

Maggie Holland 94
Tokyo, Japan

Susan L. Hoover 15
Milwaukee, Wisconsin

Judy Hooworth 118
Terrey Hills, New South Wales
Australia

Sara Hotchkiss 19
Portland, Maine

Linda Hough 68
Laguna Beach, California

Suzanne Housley 79
Barrington, Rhode Island

Constance Hunt 15
San Francisco, California

Ann W. Hyman 180, 181
Portland, Oregon

I

B. Ingram-Bartholamaus 139
Berlin, West Germany

Betty E. Ives 116
Windsor, Ontario, Canada

J

Carrie Jacobson 157
Capitola, California

Victor Jacoby 18
Eureka, California

Lucy A. Jahns 152
Libertyville, Illinois

Wanda Clayton James 48
Memphis, Tennessee

Louise Jamet 80, 163
Laval, Quebec, Canada

Jan Janeiro 65
Oakland, California

Hyun Mi Jang 43, 44
Warren, Michigan

Lis Jensen 145
Vancouver, British Columbia, Canada

Margot Strand Jensen 140, 173
Aurora, Colorado

Rosita Johanson 158
Toronto, Ontario, Canada

Dean Johns 22
Charlotte, North Carolina

David L. Johnson 31
Chicago, Illinois

Linda Nelson Johnson 137, 177
Chandler, Arizona

Sandra Kay Johnson 14
Arroyo Grande, California

Ann Johnston 112
Lake Oswego, Oregon

Mary Anne Jordan 67
Lawrence, Kansas

K

Judy L. Kahle 149
Wauseon, Ohio

Virginia Kaiser 102
North Adelaide, South Australia

Jeannie Kamins 57
Vancouver, British Columbia, Canada

Jean L. Kares 70
Vancouver, British Columbia, Canada

Pirkko Karvonen 55
Sherwood Park, Alberta, Canada

Linda Kaun 148
Los Angeles, California

Alison Keenan 13
Vancouver, British Columbia, Canada

Susan Kelly 24
Calgary, Alberta, Canada

Maureen Kelman 73
Providence, Rhode Island

Charlotte Kennedy 160
Vancouver, British Columbia, Canada

Kathleen L. Kent 27
Bridgeport, New York

Lotte Kent 175
Swarthmore, Pennsylvania

Sandra Kessler 143
Wheeling, Illinois

Patricia A. Killoran 56
Syracuse, New York

Gloria Kim 144
Williamston, Michigan

Connie Kindahl 50
Pelham, Massachusetts

Suzanne Kjelland 112
Gig Harbor, Washington

Barbara Klaer 179, 185
New Albany, Ohio

Judith Klaer 179, 185
New Albany, Ohio

M.A. Klein 115
Alamo, California

Susanne Klinke 167
Muenster, West Germany

Katherine Knauer 134, 135
New York, New York

Keiko Kobayashi 80, 194
Tokyo, Japan

Ellen Kochansky 138
Pickens, South Carolina

Joan L. Kopchik 87
Southampton, Pennsylvania

Dr. N. Zimmerman Kotch 195
Dallas, Texas

Denise Marie Kraft 38
Dahlonega, Georgia

Rita Kriege 74
Nurnberg, West Germany

Lilo Kruse 127
Kevelaer, West Germany

L

Christine T. Laffer 11, 12
San Jose, California

Doreen Lah 146
Garland, Texas

Louise Landry 186
New York, New York

Shereen La Plantz 103
Bayside, California

Judith Larzelere 119, 131
Dedham, Massachusetts

Carol S. Lasnier 109
Hebron, Connecticut

Carol Lavine 54
Point-Richmond, California

Sue Lawty 33
Hebden Bridge, West Yorkshire England

Iran Lawrence 111
Newark, Delaware

Ulrika Leander 30, 34
Oak Ridge, Tennessee

Patti Lechman 104
Memphis, Tennessee

Connie Lehman 156
Elizabeth, Colorado

Libby Lehman 120
Houston, Texas

Karen Leitch 19
Regina, Saskatchewan, Canada

Janice Lessman-Moss 61
Ravenna, Ohio

Janet Leszczynski 163
Chicago, Illinois

Wendy Lewington 135
Clearbrook, British Columbia, Canada

Robin S. Lewis 80
Mineral Bluff, Georgia

Boyana H. Leznicki 31
Verona, New Jersey

Erica Licea-Kane 152
Arlington, Massachusetts

Lore Lindenfeld 60
Princeton, New Jersey

Donna L. Lish 77
Clinton, New Jersey

Ellen Liss 191
Arlington, Massachusetts

Linda Lochmiller 168
Chicago, Illinois

Roslyn Logsdon 159
Laurel, Maryland

Janet Long 193
Lincoln Park, Michigan

Dana Loud 31
Rochester, New York

Doris Louie 50, 192
Albuquerque, New Mexico

Cindy Lowther 16
Alexandria, Virginia

M

Renate Maak 93
Graz, Austria

Marleah Drexler MacDougal 83
The Woodlands, Texas

Barbara Macey 139
Mt. Waverley, Victoria, Australia

Ilona Mack 24
New York, New York

Barbara MacLeod 70
Willowdale, Ontario, Canada

Dawn Macnutt 78
Dartmouth, Nova Scotia, Canada

Patricia Malarcher 66
Englewood, New Jersey

Anthea Mallinson 20
West Vancouver, British Columbia, Canada

Audrey Mann 98
Belmont, Massachusetts

Ruth C. Manning 17
Rochester, New York

Sharon Marcus 25
Portland, Oregon

Marcel Marois 10
Quebec City, Quebec, Canada

Jane Marshall-Wild 148
Lindsay, Ontario, Canada

Donna Martin 29
Santa Fe, New Mexico

Bobby Lynn Maslen 113
West Linn, Oregon

Fran Mather 48
Asheville, North Carolina

Salley Mavor 158, 159
Woods Hole, Massachusetts

Kathryn Maxwell 96
Detroit, Michigan

Sine McCann 42, 174
Bunbury, Western Australia, Australia

Carol Anne McComb 96
Port Ludlow, Washington

Julie McCracken 26
Irvine, California

Moyra McNeill 163
West Wickham, Kent,
England

Claudia Mederer 25
Kleedorf, West Germany

Diane Shierry Meier 83
Batavia, Illinois

Ursula Mennerich 184
Munich, West Germany

J. Michaels-Paque 74
Milwaukee, Wisconsin

Constance Miller 86
Edwardsville, Illinois

Margaret J. Miller 133
San Marcos, California

Ann Newdigate Mills 32
Saskatoon, Sask.,
Canada

Norma Minkowitz 79
Westport, Connecticut

Akiko Mio 104
Saitama, Japan

Patti Mitchem 47
S. Berwick, Maine

Beverly Moor 81
Highland Park, Illinois

Dottie Moore 116
Rock Hill, South Carolina

Jennifer Moore 43, 68
Santa Barbara, California

Marilyn Moore 102
Seattle, Washington

Susan M. Moran 148
Ann Arbor, Michigan

Robin Morey 132
Harrow, Ontario, Canada

Dennis E. Morris 94
Springfield, Illinois

Zoe Morrow 97
Moorestown, New Jersey

Barbara J. Mortenson 132
Melrose Park, Pennsylvania

Star Moxley 168
Boise, Idaho

Monika Mueller 201
Dusseldorf, West Germany

Judy Mulford 99
Los Angeles, California

Robin E. Muller 62
Halifax, Nova Scotia,
Canada

Clare Murray 118, 123
Parma, Ohio

Jo-Ann Murray 129
Cambridge, Massachusetts

N

Midori Nagai 35, 36
Toronto, Ontario, Canada

Dominie Nash 118
Bethesda, Maryland

Charles Neely 92
Columbia, Missouri

Cynthia Neely 47, 51
Madison, Connecticut

Mary Newsome 148
Toorak, Victoria, Australia

Laura Foster Nicholson 56
Houston, Texas

Marty Noble 141, 146
Ojai, California

Pam Norman 71
Dundas, Ontario, Canada

Patricia Wilmott Novarr 181
Ithaca, New York

O

Leena O'Connor 44
Taos, New Mexico

Paul R. O'Connor 72
St. Paul, Minnesota

Judith Olney 99, 101
Rowley, Massachusetts

Ira Ono 192
Volcano, Hawaii

Martha Donovan Opdahl 157
Greencastle, Indiana

Susan Osmond 201
East Aurora, New York

Carol Owen 90, 91
Jacksonville, Florida

Sherry Owens 37
Dallas, Texas

P

Janet Page-Kessler 122
New York, New York

Sharron Parker 93
Raleigh, North Carolina

Esther Parkhurst 129
Los Angeles, California

Susan Pauley 60
N. Liberty, Iowa

Liv Pedersen 11
Calgary, Alberta, Canada

Tery Pellettier 147
Toronto, Ontario, Canada

Linda Elsa Perala 149
Memphis, Tennessee

Rise Andersen
Petersons 105, 110
Cashton, Wisconsin

Gugger Petter 17
San Rafael, California

Margarete Pfaff 39
Bremen, West Germany

William A. Pope 109
Staffordville, Connecticut

Lydia Predominate 176
Rome, Italy

Nancy B. Prichard 86
Virginia Beach, Virginia

Robin Pyzik-Shuler 152
Ann Arbor, Michigan

Q

Ellen Wood Quade 54
Richmond, Virginia

Sarah Quinton 144
Toronto, Ontario, Canada

R

Pam Rajpal 132
Belmont, Massachusetts

Isis Ray 48
Seattle, Washington

Jane Reeves 125
Canton, Ohio

Myra Reichel 19
Philadelphia, Pennsylvania

Laura Munson Reinstatler 136
Seattle, Washington

Joh Ricci 58
Baltimore, Maryland

Lesley Richmond 152
Vancouver, British Columbia,
Canada

Mary Risseeuw 184
DeKalb, Illinois

Sue H. Rodgers 138
Mountain Lakes, New Jersey

Cindy K. Rogers 82
Chico, California

Leslie Rogers 147
New York, New York

Brenda Rolls 75, 189
Klenzig, South Australia
Australia

Lucretia Romey 121
E. Orleans, Massachusetts

Carol M. Rosen 95
Califon, New Jersey

Jann Rosen-Queralt 94
Baltimore, Maryland

Rebecca Ross 82
Caledon, Ontario, Canada

Jan Ross-Manley 76, 138, 164
North Dandenong, Victoria
Australia

Kristin Carlsen Rowley 28
Syracuse, New York

Antoinette Roy 86
Quebec, Canada

Dona Rozanski 43
Seattle, Washington

Deann Joy Rubin 11
Chesterfield, Missouri

S

Carole Sabiston 67
Victoria, British Columbia
Canada

Margaret Ahrens Sahlstrand 91
Ellensburg, Washington

Betz Salmont 86
Manhattan Beach, California

Denise Samuels 79, 93
Ann Arbor, Michigan

Diana Sanderson 199
Vancouver, British Columbia
Canada

Stephanie Santmyers 124
Greensboro, North Carolina

Beatrice Schall 65
Greensboro, North Carolina

Christine Schechter 150
Dearborn, Michigan

Deidre Scherer 57
Williamsville, Vermont

Lois Schklar 173
Thornhill, Ontario, Canada

Barbara Schulman 38, 64
Raleigh, North Carolina

Robin Schwalb 120
New York, New York

Hisako Sekijima 102, 107
Kanagawa, Japan

Beverly Semmons 105
Cincinnati, Ohio

A. Sempel-Kleinlosen 152
Nieblum, West Germany

H. Jeannette Shanks 115
Jackson's Point, Ontario
Canada

Sheila Sharp 190
Edinburgh, Scotland

Susan Shie 171
Wooster, Ohio

Elizabeth Sibley 88
Nantucket, Massachusetts

Julie Silletti 182
S. Milwaukee, Wisconsin

A. de la Mauviniere Silva 133
Ottawa, Ontario, Canada

Barbara Simon 197, 198
St. Louis, Missouri

Louisa Simons 195
Parnell, Auckland
New Zealand

Audrey Simpson 107
North Ryde, New South Wales,
Australia

John L. Skau 69, 178
Lansing, Michigan

Susan Sloane 100
Conway, New Hampshire

Louise Slobodan 142, 143
Vancouver, British Columbia,
Canada

Elaine Small 106
Ferguson, Missouri

C. Elizabeth Smathers 19
Nashville, Tennessee

Carter Smith 154
Nahant, Massachusetts

Elly Smith 166
Seattle, Washington

Sherri Smith 46
Ann Arbor, Michigan

Joanne Soroka 37
Edinburgh, Scotland

Patricia Spark 90
Albany, Oregon

Kathy Spoering 34
Grand Junction, Colorado

Georgia M. Springer 118
Raleigh, North Carolina

Maria J. Stachowska 85
Richmond, Surrey,
England

Care Standley 14
Berkeley, California

Dianne Stanton 98
Pembroke, Massachusetts

Aafke Stavenga 45
Bedum, The Netherlands

Lynn Stearns 156
Yorkville, Illinois

Judith Stein 187
Rochester, New York

Dilys Stinson 28
Hawkhurst, Kent, England

Marilyn Stothers 136
Winnipeg, Manitoba,
Canada

Meredith Strauss 71
Glendale, California

Beryl Stutchbury 146
Belair, South Australia,
Australia

Florence Suerig 74
Greenwich, Connecticut

Helen Suits 142
Gainesville, Florida

Gabrielle Sutt 18, 35
Toronto, Ontario,, Canada

Tina Sutton 17
St. Lucia, Queensland,
Australia

Lynne Sward 127, 131
Virginia Beach, Virginia

Astri Raestad Synnes 163
Vigra, Norway

Norma Szumski 20
Richmond, Virginia

T

Anthony Tate 65
Memphis, Tennessee

Nola Taylor 136
Sydney, New South Wales,
Australia

Jan Taylor-Taskey 123
Vancouver, Washington

Char TerBeest 105
Baraboo, Wisconsin

Vebjorg Hagene Thoe 114
Vestresand, Norway

Stephen Thurston 12
Chicago, Illinois

Elmyra Tidwell 193
Hermann, Missouri

Judith Tinkl 126
Sunderland, Ontario,
Canada

Mary Towner 87
Boalsburg, Pennsylvania

Steven Tucker 73
Philadelphia, Pennsylvania

Michele Tuegel 85
Clearwater, Florida

Kaija Tyni-Rautiainen 54
Burnaby, British Columbia,
Canada

U

Andrea V. Uravitch 176
Arlington, Virginia

V

Jana Vander Lee 55
Houston, Texas

Betty Vera 53
New York, New York

W

Carol Ann Wadley 120
Hillsboro, Oregon

Barbara Walker 41, 51
Toronto, Ontario, Canada

Judy Anne Walter 127
Chicago, Illinois

Judi Warren 122
Maumee, Ohio

Sue Watson 176
Avalon, New South Wales
Australia

Judith A. Weiss 124, 125
Peoria, Illinois

Elisabeth Weissensteiner 167
Vienna, Austria

Leanne Weissler 84
New Rochelle, New York

Ann Welch 188
Brooklyn, New York

Deane M. Wernet 27
Mountain View, California

Gina Westergard 194
San Diego, California

Patricia Wheeler 191
Berkeley, California

Judi Maureen White 31
Tempe, Arizona

Patricia White 130
San Francisco, California

Susan D. Wilchins 44
Raleigh, North Carolina

Sunhild Wollwage 56, 59
Mauren,
Principality of Liechtenstein

Lynnie Wonfor 115
Calgary, Alberta, Canada

Vera K. Worling 39
Aurora, Ontario, Canada

Kathy Wosika 88
Fresno, California

Sandi Wright 188
Albuquerque, New Mexico

Y

Joce Yanni 184, 188
San Diego, California

Soui Yoon 61
Ann Arbor, Michigan

Martha Stilwell Young 137
Cleveland Heights, Ohio

Z

Emily Zopf 126
Olympia, Washington

(E) Del Zoppo 48
Cape Breton, Nova Scotia,
Canada